The Forgotten Soldiers

The Forgotten Soldiers

DECEASED U.S. MILITARY PERSONNEL IN THE WAR WITH MEXICO

MONUMENT TO THE AMERICANS.

STEVEN R. BUTLER

Poor Scholar Publications

Richardson, Texas

Poor Scholar Publications

ISBN 978-0-9981526-2-2

For information about Poor Scholar titles, please visit:
www.watermelon-kid.com/poorscholar/psp.htm

Additional copies of this book are available from:
Amazon.com and other online stores

Contents

Preface

(**Author's Note:** Apart from the Epilogue and some corrections and minor revisions, the chapters in this book—including this preface—are the same as the Master's thesis I wrote while a graduate student at the University of Texas at Arlington in 1999.)

During the mid-1990s, on behalf of the Descendants of Mexican War Veterans—a non-profit, non-political, national lineage society of which I was then an officer—I began compiling a list of names of U.S. military personnel who were casualties of the War with Mexico. This task was performed with a view to the future publication of a book that might be of interest and value to historians and genealogists alike.

Even before I began compiling this data, I was acutely aware that after nearly one hundred and fifty years, most of these men still lay buried in lost and neglected graves in Mexico, in places that were never visited by their loved ones, seemingly forgotten by the government that they had faithfully served. I felt that this was not only a tragedy but a national disgrace and I determined to write an essay, to accompany the list I was compiling, that would tell what I saw as a particularly sad story.

Owing to the need to attend to more pressing obligations I was unable to find the time to write my proposed essay, but after I became enrolled in graduate school at the University of Texas at Arlington in the fall of 1997 it occurred to me that the story of these "forgotten soldiers" might possibly be acceptable material for a master's thesis. When I first discussed the possibility with Dr. Gerald Saxon during the summer of 1998 he agreed that it seemed suitable. Later, when I proposed the subject at my first consultation with Dr. Sam Haynes, my thesis committee chairman, he also agreed and not only consented but encouraged me go ahead. Thus I was enabled, as the old saying goes, "to kill two birds with one stone."

At the outset, however, my advisors cautioned me to refrain from allowing my intense personal interest in the subject to intrude. They reminded me that I needed to write an objective historical paper, not an editorial. I took that advice to heart and I hope that my readers will agree that I have followed it

Because there were no previous studies of this subject (or certainly none that I could locate), I relied heavily on primary sources. I began by examining the published diaries, letters, and recollections of soldiers, looking for accounts of funerals and burials at battle sites and other places in Mexico where U.S. troops were stationed. I also consulted rosters and muster rolls of U.S. military organizations. Period newspapers were helpful as well.

To tell the story of the establishment of the Mexico City National Cemetery, I turned to diplomatic correspondence between the State Department and the U.S. ministry in Mexico City. The *Congressional Globe* and *U.S. Statutes at Large* were likewise helpful. Other diplomatic correspondence provided information about the investigations of American burial sites in Saltillo and Monterey. Publications of the National Association of Veterans of the Mexican War were useful too.

My central argument, that when compared to U.S. soldiers who died in other foreign wars, those who fell in Mexico have been singularly neglected, is well supported by the evidence: The many federal statutes that have been passed since 1898 and the records of the American Battle Monuments Commission. My conclusion, which attempts to explain why the U.S. government has seemingly forgotten about these earlier soldiers, is admittedly speculative but not at all implausible. In the absence of any official explanation, I believe it is the best that can be hoped for at the present time.

Acknowledgements

No historian works completely alone and I am no exception. Certainly, I would be remiss if I did not acknowledge the many individuals whose advice, encouragement and assistance proved invaluable to me. First, for long ago encouraging me to return to school to pursue a graduate degree, I want to thank Ms. Marcelle Hull, who has since retired from her position as archivist in the Special Collections Division of the University of Texas at Arlington Library, Dr. Gerald Saxon, who still heads that department, and Judge David Jackson of the Summerlee Foundation, a long-time friend and mentor.

For donating his private collection of Mexican War materials to the University of Texas at Arlington, I am grateful to the late Mr. Jenkins Garrett. For helping me make the most of Mr. Garrett's generosity, I wish to thank a researcher's best friend, Ms. Kit Goodwin.

Thanks are also due to all the professors under whom I studied from 1997 to 1999: Dr. Richard Francaviglia, Dr. Jerry Rodnitzky, Dr. Stephanie Cole, Dr. Kathleen Underwood, Dr. Chris Morris, Dr. Robert Fairbanks, and Dr. Stephen Maizlish.

Grateful thanks are also extended to Dr. Bruce Winders at the Alamo and especially to Dr. Sam Haynes, Dr. Douglas Richmond, and Dr. Gerald Saxon for their advice, their encouragement, and for agreeing to serve on my thesis committee.

Thanks are also due to my wife Anita, who put up with my ignoring her for hours on end while I sat in front of my computer typing!

A wounded soldier; from an old engraving (source uncertain).

Chapter 1
The Forgotten Soldiers

One of the tragic consequences of any war is that soldiers die. This is a universal truth that people distanced from such events by time, a group that includes historians, seem to take for granted. Armies do not have this luxury. For reasons of both health and simple humanity, a body-strewn battleground or a field hospital filled with dead and dying soldiers cannot be long ignored. The prompt disposal of remains, in particular, by whatever methods are deemed appropriate according to both custom and official policy, is something to which all armies must attend. In this respect, the United States Army in the War with Mexico was certainly no exception. Between 1846 and 1848, more than 13,000 U.S. military personnel lost their lives. Most, as statistics prove and the majority of historians of this period point out, were the victims of illness and disease. What to do with them was a reality that both Gen. Zachary Taylor and Gen. Winfield Scott, the two leading U.S. military commanders of this conflict, frequently had to face.

Despite the regularity with which this melancholy duty was performed, or perhaps on account of it, battle reports and dispatches composed by Taylor, Scott, and others, are remarkably silent on the subject. The diaries, letters, and recollections of American soldiers, however, are not. Most of the officers and enlisted men who were literate seem also to have been sensitive, reflective individuals. The untimely demise of a fellow soldier was not taken lightly. "Dreadful hour to him, all important awful hour to him!" lamented Capt. Franklin Smith in his journal, sorrowing also for "those dear innocents sleeping in peace and quiet on the banks of the Illinois, the

1

Wabash, the Ohio, the Missi[ssippi], the Cumberland, or the Alabama, and dreaming they will soon see their pa."[1]

Occasionally, letters and journal entries also included an account of a soldier's funeral, as well as some brief description of the unfortunate fellow's burial place. Reading such documents more than one hundred and seventy years later, it is clear that at least some of the men who wrote them realized that they were doing two things that no other American soldiers had ever done before: Not only were they fighting a war almost entirely within the bounds of another country, they were also interring the bodies of their deceased comrades in the soil of their declared enemy. Furthermore, compelled by circumstances and in the absence of any lawful mandate requiring them to do otherwise, they left them there, in places where no family member was ever likely to visit. They knew this was unusual. In all previous U.S. wars, the families of fallen soldiers could take some comfort in the knowledge that their loved one had at least been buried in his native soil, if not at home. Many Mexican War veterans would live to see the day when federal legislation would permit the families of soldiers who died in subsequent foreign wars to enjoy that same consolation.

From the beginning, the government's lack of any policy regarding the remains of deceased military personnel during the years 1846-1848 seems to have been the cause of no little trepidation among those whom it most closely affected, namely the soldiers themselves. One was Col. William Ryan Curtis, commander of the 3d Regiment of Ohio Volunteers. On a warm October evening in 1846, Curtis sat in his tent on the south bank of the Rio Grande and wrote in the journal that he had been keeping faithfully since July 3, the date he and his men had departed on the first leg of a journey that had taken them from Cincinnati to U.S.-occupied Matamoros. From time to time, a northerly breeze came gusting in through the open tent flap, providing a welcome but fleeting respite from the heat that

---

[1] Joseph E. Chance, *The Mexican War Journal of Captain Franklin Smith* (Jackson: University Press of Mississippi, 1991), 111.

caused the 41-year-old officer to "perspire freely." After detailing the day's events in his book, which Curtis complained was "composed of miserable paper and cost a dollar as poor as it is," he turned his hand to sketching a plan of the Mexican border town where the soldiers from Ohio had been stationed since August 18. On this map he marked the site of their encampment, carefully noting the alignment of each company's row of tents. At three locations, two beside the Ohioans' campsite and the third near the center of the city, he drew crosses to represent "the places where the dead have been deposited."[2]

"It is to these," Curtis reflected, "that we have often had to follow the slow hearse and muffled drum." Expressing what seems to have been an almost universal sentiment, he added poignantly: "It will be hard to leave these graves in possession of our foes. The places will no doubt soon be lost and forgotten, and mourning friends will find no trace of these graves."[3]

Other soldiers have left evidence that they were equally disturbed by the necessity of leaving the remains of a fallen comrade behind, buried in an anonymous "soldier's grave," where he would be "forgotten by all his friends and but those dear to him by the law of nature."[4] One man, who had perhaps seen too many men consigned to unmarked graves, wrote cynically: "Suppose you are killed, will your country mourn your loss? Pshaw! Nobody but the little home circle will remember that you ever lived six months hence."[5]

Undoubtedly, the government's policy of leaving soldiers' remains buried in enemy territory unsettling was unsettling to

---

[2] Joseph E. Chance, *Mexico Under Fire: Being the Diary of Samuel Ryan Curtis, 3d Ohio Volunteer Regiment, During the American Military Occupation of Northern Mexico, 1846-1847* (Fort Worth: Texas Christian University Press, 1994), 44-45.

[3] Ibid.

[4] D. E. Livingston-Little, *The Mexican War Diary of Thomas D. Tennery* (Norman, Oklahoma: University of Oklahoma Press, 1970), 22.

[5] Richard M'Sherry, *El Puchero* (Philadelphia: Lippincott, Grambo, & Co., 1850), 41.

civilians, particularly those who formed "the little home circle." On several occasions, dead soldiers were disinterred from their battlefield graves in Mexico and transported home at the expense of family, friends, or community. This task was not only difficult and costly but also potentially hazardous. There is at least one instance on record of a special agent, sent to Mexico to retrieve the bodies of several deceased officers, who contracted a fatal disease, probably at Vera Cruz. When he died at New Orleans, while performing his duty, his body was forwarded home with the remains of the men he had been sent to collect.

In the event that the cost of transportation could be met, finding the remains of a specific individual after he had been buried seems to have presented the greatest challenge. Unless the soldier's grave had been marked or there was someone in his regiment who could identify the burial site, there was probably little chance that he could be located. Finding the bodies of junior officers and enlisted men seem to have presented the most difficulty. Men who died in battle were often buried in mass graves. Even when a man was interred individually, his grave was not always identified and when it was, a wooden stake or rude wooden cross was frequently the marker of both choice and necessity. Therein lay the problem. Wind and rain could cause these to fall over. Without any other visible signs, after several weeks or months, following the settling of the soil and the re-growth of vegetation, a grave might become indistinguishable from its surroundings. Hastily dug graves were not only badly marked they were often shallow as well. In some instances ravenous wild animals dug up the remains of recently buried soldiers and feasted upon them. Grave looters looking for clothing or valuables were another possible problem. The coffin of one American officer, including his body, was stolen from a church in Puebla and was never found. These circumstances no doubt discouraged some families from even attempting to bring home the remains of a husband, son, or father.

In contrast to the graves of enlisted men, the burial sites of senior or well-liked officers seem, as a rule, to have been well marked, in some cases in anticipation of the body being later disinterred. It appears that the more distinguished or popular an officer had been in life, the more likely he was to be reburied in his native soil. The families of such men, or their friends or communities, were also more likely to have the money to pay for the expense of having the fallen soldier's remains brought home. Owing to their notoriety, for example, it is hardly surprising that Col. Archibald Yell, the former governor of Arkansas, Col. John J. Hardin, a former Illinois congressman, and Lt. Col. Henry Clay, Jr., son of the distinguished statesman whose name he shared, all of whom were killed in the Battle of Buena Vista, did not remain buried in their graves in Saltillo for very long.

Stirred by feelings of national pride, even civilians who were not directly affected by the loss of a son, a father, or a husband seem to have believed that the government was remiss in its failure to fulfill what is now commonly regarded as a national obligation. One such person was Teresa Griffin Vielé, the wife of a young army lieutenant stationed at Ringgold Barracks, Texas. During the early 1850s, Mrs. Vielé visited the battlefield of Palo Alto. She was struck, she later wrote, by its peaceful appearance, finding it difficult to imagine that the broad expanse of coastal prairie that lay before her had once been "associated with the sound of booming guns, gallant charges, and groans of wounded and dying men." Sitting atop her horse, gazing upon a scene "where the sounds of the wilderness alone break the stillness of the air," she became lost in thought, recalling the soldiers who lost their lives at Palo Alto and other places during the war. Afterward, when she had time to put pen to paper, Mrs. Vielé wrote:

> It seems almost a disgrace to think of the many forgotten graves of young and noble men that lie scattered everywhere. The glory conferred by them on their country seems to demand some better return. The blood stained hills and valleys of our land are the ruby jewels in the crown...if we fail to mark those spots where heroes fall with tablets that tell of their gallant deeds, it is not only wronging them, but wronging generations yet unborn, by allowing them to

forget how precious the purchase-money that bought their freedom.[6]

A little more than a decade later, following the Civil War, an article appeared in *Harper's New Monthly Magazine* that described the newly established U.S. national cemeteries at Gettysburg and other places. Although the anonymous author seemed pleased that the federal government had not "forgotten its duty [to its fallen soldiers] in our late war," he confessed he was taken aback when he learned that "it seems to have omitted it in all previous ones." During each of the nation's earlier military conflicts, the writer pointed out, soldiers who lost their lives were simply "interred on the spot where they fell and that was the last the nation knew or seemed to care for them." Calling it "neglect of our national duty," the article's author appeared to be truly astonished that in the case of soldiers who perished in previous wars, "nothing approaching to the dignity of national respect or national care appears ever to have been manifested afterward."[7]

Although he failed to distinguish between U.S. soldiers who were buried in their native soil, such as those who perished during the American Revolution and the War of 1812, and those whose remains were interred within the bounds of a foreign land, as in the case of the U.S.-Mexican War, the anonymous *Harper's* writer was correct. Apart from the establishment of Mexico City National Cemetery in 1851, in which less than 6 percent of all the soldiers who died in Mexico were buried, the federal government had, up to that time, done little to fulfill its "national duty" to those who gave their lives in the service of the early republic.

Certainly, the years immediately following the Civil War saw a significant shift in the government's attitude regarding fallen soldiers, as manifested in the establishment of several national cemeteries

---

[6] Teresa Griffin Vielé, *Following the Drum: A Glimpse of Frontier Life* (New York: Rudd & Carleton, 1858; reprint ed., Lincoln, Nebraska: University of Nebraska Press, 1984), pp. 101-102.

[7] "National Cemeteries," *Harper's New Monthly Magazine*, vol. xxxiii, no. cxcv, August 1866, 312.

throughout the United States. This apparent move toward a more humanitarian outlook on the part of the national government gained momentum during the Spanish-American War, when federal legislation was passed offering the families of soldiers who died overseas the opportunity to have their loved one's remains returned home at government expense. This policy, periodically renewed and expanded during the past one hundred years, is still in place today. Where the return of remains has not been practicable, as in the case of battles resulting in large numbers of fatalities, U.S. servicemen and women have been buried in American cemeteries located in other countries, mostly notably Great Britain, France, Belgium, and the Philippines. Apart from the one in Mexico City, however, none of these overseas cemeteries are situated within the boundaries of any nations that were the declared enemies of the United States during the wars that led to their establishment.

When compared to the federal government's treatment of the remains of deceased soldiers in all subsequent foreign conflicts, the men who perished during the U.S.-Mexican War stand forth as a singularly neglected group. Providing further contrast are efforts that have been made by the federal government during recent decades to locate the remains of soldiers reported "missing-in-action" in Vietnam and Cambodia. As lately as November 1998, a newspaper reported that Defense Department teams were still "scouring remote locations in Southeast Asia, hoping to bring home the remains of those still missing from the Vietnam War," adding that since 1992, "more than 450 sets of remains believed to be Americans" had been recovered. The report noted further "the government also is actively seeking to account for missing Americans from the Korean War and those who disappeared during the Cold War."[8] Why the federal government has not done the same for its soldiers who lie buried within the bounds of a country that is not only much closer to the United States than Korea or Vietnam but actually shares a border

---

[8] "Hope Not Forgotten," *The Dallas Morning News*, Dallas, Texas, November 29, 1998, 1A & 20A.

with it is a question for which no easy answer is forthcoming.

One reason for the government's apparent inaction, it might be imagined, is that after the passage of so many years, it has simply not known where to look for the remains of U.S. soldiers in Mexico. This may be partly true but the location of some sites are well documented, thanks both to soldiers' writings and to no less than three government investigations that were carried out during the last quarter of the nineteenth century. The first of these, conducted in response to an inquiry from the National Association of Veterans of the Mexican War, resulted in confirmation of the location and condition of American burial sites in both Monterey[9] and Saltillo. A newspaper report on the 50th anniversary of the Battle of Buena Vista prompted a second investigation into the condition of American graves at Saltillo. Three years later, yet a third investigation was conducted at Saltillo. In all instances, however, once the information was obtained, no further action was taken. This is the mystery.

Until now, it appears that a comprehensive accounting of how and where the remains of deceased U.S. military personnel in the War with Mexico were interred has never been attempted. This may be the first and it is admittedly incomplete. In the absence of any official records of interments, it has been necessary to rely almost entirely upon muster rolls, military rosters, and the diaries, letters, and recollections of American soldiers who witnessed or participated in the burial of their fallen comrades. A compilation of quantitative data would no doubt have been a welcome component but such an undertaking was simply beyond the scope of this work.

It also appears that no one has ever before attempted to explain the vast disparity between the government's treatment of its Mexican War dead and soldiers who perished in subsequent foreign wars. This may be simply because no one has ever given it much thought. Like

---

[9] The modern-day spelling of this large city in Northern Mexico is *Monterey*. Throughout this work, however, I have chosen to use the spelling that was common at the time of the U.S.-Mexican War.

the soldiers whose bones still rest in forgotten and neglected graves from one end of Mexico to the other, the war in which they fought seems also to have been forgotten. This alone is ample evidence that Teresa Vielé's fear was realized. By failing to mark the spots where its soldiers died in the line of duty, their country has not remembered them. They have become "the forgotten soldiers."

INTERIOR OF FORT BROWN.

The Graves of Major Brown and Lieut. Stevens at the foot of the Flag staff.

Chapter 2
How and Where They Were Buried

While there may have been no legislation mandating the return of a soldier's remains to his family during the War with Mexico, U.S. Army regulations, promulgated in 1841, clearly set forth the funeral honors that were required to be paid to deceased military personnel. By way of illustration, the firing of an artillery salute was reserved for the President of the United States or a Major-General. All other officers, non-commissioned officers, and enlisted men were entitled only to a musket volley. In contrast, the size and make-up of funeral escorts varied greatly according to rank. A colonel who died in service, for instance, rated an entire regiment while a captain was entitled to a company. The escort for a private was "eight rank and file, commanded by a corporal."[10]

The funeral service for all ranks was also spelled out in detail. The escort, according to regulations, had to "be formed in two ranks, opposite to the quarters or tent of the deceased, with shouldered arms and bayonets fixed." If all were present, artillery and cavalry troops were required to be "on the right of the infantry."[11]

"Upon the appearance of the corpse," the regulations further stated, "the officer commanding the escort" was required to command them to present arms. At that point, "honors due to the deceased will be played by the drums and trumpets." Next, the body of the deceased would be "taken to the right where it will be halted." After the person commanding the escort ordered his men to shoulder

---

[10] *General Regulations, Army of the United States* (Washington, D. C.: J. & G. S. Gideon, Printers, 1841), 90-92.
[11] Ibid.

arms, the procession would commence, marching "in common time, to appropriate music."[12]

When they reached the grave, the officer or non-commissioned officer commanding the escort was required to have the soldiers present arms momentarily and then stand with shouldered arms "while the funeral service is performed." Finally, as the coffin was being lowered into the grave, the escort would be commanded to come to attention, to load their weapons and then fire three rounds over the grave, "taking care to elevate the pieces." Immediately afterward, the escort would march away in silence, until they had marched an appropriate distance, at which time the musicians would begin to play again.[13]

The regulations also prescribed that "the usual badge of military mourning, worn "when in full, or in undress" uniform was to be "a piece of black crape around the left arm, and also upon the sword-hilt."[14]

In addition to providing him with a proper funeral, the commanding officer of a deceased officer was required to report the man's death to the Adjutant General of the Army, "specifying the date of his decease," along with an inventory of his personal effects. Furthermore, stated the regulations: "If a legal administrator or family connection be present, to take charge of the effects, it will be so stated to the Adjutant General."[15]

The rules regarding deceased enlisted men were even more detailed than those that applied to officers. Not only was it required for the soldier's death to be reported to his commanding officer but also "the date, place, and cause; to what time he was last paid, and the money or other effects in his possession at the time of his decease." This information, stated the regulations, had to be "noted on the next

---

[12] Ibid.
[13] Ibid.
[14] Ibid.
[15] Ibid, 21-22.

muster roll of the company to which the man belonged."[16]

Although it appears that soldiers' deaths were recorded in conformity with regulations throughout the war, adherence to the directives regarding funeral formalities seems to have varied according to circumstances. At places where casualties were light and there was plenty of time for niceties to be observed, the regulations were followed to the letter. Where deaths were frequent and men grew weary of hearing the firing of a volley over some unfortunate man's grave, "proper" funeral services seem to have been seen by some men as a waste of time and effort. Other soldiers' sensibilities were offended by this attitude. When General Scott, reputed to be a "by-the-book" man, learned in January 1847 that regulation funerals were not being given to many of the deceased soldiers who died in army hospitals in Mexico City, he issued the following general order:

> It is represented that some of our gallant men who have recently died, in general hospital, have not been buried with due solemnity. The General-in-Chief is certain that no blame can be attached either to the Chaplains of the Army or to the Catholic priests of the city. On due notice they, no doubt, would promptly have performed the duties of their holy offices at the graves of the deceased.
>
> It is ordered that the body of no soldier, no matter what his rank, if not executed as a felon, shall be buried in future, without the customary military honors, unless the presence of the enemy may render the ceremony impracticable, and also without giving notice to some clergyman, at hand, according to the religion of the deceased.
>
> Patients who die in general hospital will be promptly reported, by the senior Surgeon of the hospital, to Brig. General Smith, if the deceased belongs to the regular army, or to the senior officer of volunteers present, if the deceased be a volunteer, who, respectively, will take care to make all proper arrangements for the funerals.[17]

Scott's order, published in the *Daily American Star*, an occupation

---

[16] Ibid.

[17] *Daily American Star* (Mexico City), January 21, 1848, 2.

newspaper printed in Mexico City, was accompanied by an editorial that applauded the General's action. "There is reason to believe," remarked the anonymous writer, "that in some instances our gallant men have been shamefully neglected in this respect." Some men, the author commented further, "have [been] known…to be placed in the ground without even a box to enclose their remains." The editorialist concluded by adding that Scott deserved "the warm thanks and commendation of every one connected with the service for the step he has taken."[18]

In addition to differences in funeral honors, in matters not specifically addressed by army regulations the remains of officers seem to have been generally treated with more consideration than those of enlisted men. More often than not, they were interred separately while the bodies of ordinary soldiers were consigned to mass graves. At Monterey, following the battle of September 21-23, 1846, a cemetery exclusively for officers was constructed by enlisted men who doubtless grumbled about it. The bodies of officers seem to have been disinterred and reburied in the United States more often as well, but this had little or nothing to do with the army. As a rule, officers tended to come from more affluent families who either had some standing in their community or had the means to pay for such services to be performed—or both.

Whether officers or enlisted men were buried in coffins depended on the availability of wooden planks to make them. Frequently, there simply weren't any. In such cases, men were consigned to what was termed a "soldier's grave," buried in what they were wearing when they died and wrapped in their blanket.

The places where soldiers were buried also depended upon circumstances. Men who died in battle were usually interred on or near the battlefield itself, and as quickly as possible. In the warm climate in which most of the war was fought, this was necessary on account of the rapidity with which decomposition could set in. Those who passed away in hospitals usually found a grave within a short

[18] Ibid, 3.

distance of whatever building they had died in. In some cases men were interred in a hastily established burial ground beside an existing Mexican cemetery, which were as a rule, reserved for Roman Catholics. This generally suited the Americans fine. Most U.S. soldiers were Protestants and many were anti-Catholic. Such men would have no more thought of burying one of their comrades inside the boundaries of a "Papist" cemetery than the Mexicans would have thought to allow it. Of course, soldiers who were of the Roman Catholic faith—and there were many owing to the high proportion of European immigrants in the U.S. Army—had no such qualms. Indeed, there were several instances of the remains of such men being interred in Mexican cemeteries, along with the appropriate Roman Catholic ceremonies.

It would probably be safe to say that at any place in Mexico and its borderlands through which U.S. soldiers passed, or where they were camped or stationed for any length of time, there are American graves or burial grounds. What's uncertain in many cases is the precise or even approximate location of these places of interment and how many soldiers were buried at each one.

This uncertainty is the result of an apparent lack of official records. Although the names of deceased soldiers were required to be entered on the muster rolls of each company during its term of service, the federal government seems not to have insisted upon the army keeping an accounting of where the bodies of these men were interred. After the war, the government was able to compile and publish reasonably accurate statistics that showed how many men served and how many of that number died in uniform, and even whether their deaths resulted from battle wounds or from illness, but had nothing, so it seems, to enable it to identify the actual spots where the bodies of these men were laid to rest. If in fact such records ever existed, they seem to have either been lost or misplaced. In the absence of official data, the only alternatives are the diaries, letters, and recollections of surviving soldiers who witnessed burials or other persons who may have had knowledge of the sites.

The U.S.-Mexican War took place in three broad areas: Texas and Northern Mexico; the West—principally the present-day states of California and New Mexico; and Central Mexico, specifically a broad band of territory commencing at Vera Cruz and extending west to the capital and encompassing a number of outlying districts. Reference to rosters, muster rolls, and general histories of the war readily yield the names of the towns and cities transited by U.S. troops in addition to the places where they were camped or formed a garrison. The following is a list of those towns and cities, by region, along with descriptions, where they could be found, of the burial sites of U.S. soldiers. In some cases, an estimate of the number of men that were interred at a particular place is also included.

TEXAS AND NORTHERN MEXICO

Corpus Christi, Texas

U.S. troops under the command of Gen. Zachary Taylor were stationed in Texas as early as July 1845. The largest number were camped at Corpus Christi, on a beach near the mouth of the Rio Nueces. Smaller groups, principally dragoons, were stationed at Austin and San Antonio.[19]

The "Army of Occupation," as it was styled, had been sent to Texas even before its annexation by the United States had been formally concluded, as a response to Mexican threats to reclaim its former province by force of arms. During the nearly eight months they spent camped at Corpus Christi, both General Taylor and his men believed that they might be attacked at any moment.[20] As events transpired, no U.S. soldiers were killed by Mexicans during this brief period although some did die, as a consequence of illness or

---

[19] *Corpus Christi Gazette*, February 5, 1846, 1.
[20] Justin Smith, *The War with Mexico*, vol. 1 (New York: The Macmillan Company, 1919; reprint ed., Gloucester, Mass.: Peter Smith, 1963), 87-88, 106-107, & 143.

accidents. It may be arguable, therefore, whether any of these men qualify as casualties of the U.S.-Mexican War. At least one of Taylor's officers thought so. Regardless, the first, and undoubtedly the best-chronicled of these early fatalities, were the soldiers who were killed in the explosion of the steamboat *Dayton*—an incident that led to the founding of the first U.S. military cemetery in Texas.

Owing to the sandbars that blocked deep-draft vessels from entering Corpus Christi Bay, General Taylor found it necessary to establish a supply depot on nearby St. Joseph's or San José Island where he and his men had first come ashore in Texas in July 1845. It was here that supplies and troops arriving from the United States were off-loaded for further transportation. The *Dayton* was a private vessel that had been leased by the Army to ferry both passengers and cargo between the island and Taylor's encampment on Corpus Christi Bay.[21]

The *Dayton*, Capt. William S. Henry of the 3rd Infantry later lamented, "was an old hulk of a thing, totally unfit to carry passengers" but was "our only choice in the absence of proper transportation." At mid-day on September 12, 1845, the vessel cast off from the camp at Corpus Christi with several soldiers aboard. At 12:20 p.m., just as the *Dayton* was passing McGloin's Bluff on the opposite side of the bay, its boilers exploded, "sending eight souls," wrote Captain Henry, "and possibly more, into eternity."[22]

"Just before the explosion," he later recalled, "Lieutenant [Thaddeus] Higgins [of the 4th Infantry]...was sitting talking to Doctor [Henry E.] Crittenden and Lieutenants [Benjamin A.] Berry [of the 4th Infantry] and [James S.] Woods [of the 2nd Infantry] were lying down near them, the former asleep, all being in the small cabin aft the social hall." Several other officers, he noted, were "standing on the boiler deck." When the first boiler suddenly burst in a fierce

---

[21] William S. Henry, *Campaign Sketches of the War with Mexico* (New York: Harper & Brothers, 1847), 17, 31; Henry Montgomery, *The Life of Major-General Zachary Taylor* (Auburn, New York: Derby, Miller & Co., 1849), 75.
[22] Henry, 35-37.

eruption of scalding steam and shattered, screaming metal, everyone outside was "blown high into the air, and were thrown into the water some distance from the boat." At almost the same moment, the boat's second boiler "was thrown into the water, and exploded with a crash like thunder." Miraculously, only a few of the men who were blasted off the deck of the *Dayton* suffered any wounds, and in most cases these were slight. Most emerged from their violent and sudden dunking completely uninjured. The recently-married Lieutenant Higgins was not so lucky, wrote Captain Henry. He was "killed immediately by a piece of iron striking him on the head." Lieutenant Berry also perished. Those who suffered the worst wounds and died later, "were horrible in the extreme to look at." Some, recalled Henry, had "nearly all the flesh off" while others were "perfectly blackened." "One negro," he remembered, was "not only scalded, but his flesh burned to a crisp." That evening, the surgeons did what little they could to ease the suffering of the injured men whose agonizing condition, recalled Henry, "would rend the heart of the most indifferent."[23]

Assigned the task of making funeral arrangements for the *Dayton's* first eight victims (a ninth died later), Lt. Col. Ethan Allen Hitchcock of the 3rd Infantry Regiment selected for a burial ground, a plot of land located "on the brow of a hill northwest of the camp" that afforded "a view of the Nueces and Corpus Christi Bay." He pronounced it "a beautiful spot." In a letter to his young wife, Lt. Napoleon Dana of the 7th Infantry Regiment agreed with Hitchcock, calling the site "romantic" and "a charming place for a cemetery"[24]

---

[23] Ibid; *The Enquirer* (Dover, New Hampshire), September 30, 1845, 3; Francis B. Heitman, *Historical Register and Dictionary of the United States Army*, vol. 1 (Washington, D.C.: U.S. Government Printing Office, 1903; reprint ed., Urbana, Illinois: University of Illinois Press, 1963), 214 & 1058; Steven R. Butler, *A Complete Roster of Mexican War Officers* (Richardson, Texas: Descendants of Mexican War Veterans, 1994), 4.

[24] W. A. Croffut, *Fifty Years in Camp and Field: Diary of Major-General Ethan Allen Hitchcock, U.S.A.* (New York and London: G. P. Putnam's Sons, 1909), 202; Robert H. Ferrell, ed., *Monterrey is Ours! The Mexican War Letters of Lt. Dana, 1845-1847* (Lexington, Kentucky: The University Press of Kentucky, 1990), 12.

The funeral, held on the evening of September 13, 1845, was especially moving. Lieutenant Dana told his wife that "tears almost came to my eyes as I wished you could be here to witness the scene on that sacred evening." The service was also well-remembered by Captain Henry, who wrote descriptively:

> From some unavoidable delay, the procession did not take up its line of march until after sunset. It was a solemn, sad march; and the circumstances and the time rendered it very impressive. The sun had just set; the clouds, piled up in pyramids, were tinged with golden light; flashes of lightning were seen in the north; the pale moon, in the east, was smiling sweetly forth, seemingly regardless of the sad feelings of those in that solemn funeral procession. They were buried about a half a mile from camp, on the top of a beautiful bluff, commanding an extensive and picturesque view. The service of the dead was read by the light of a lamp. Three volleys were fired over their graves. The escort wheeled into column, and, to a lively air from fife and drum, we left the soldiers to their long sleep, and their dreary but romantic graves.[25]

It is likely that any soldiers who died of illness during the nearly eight months that Taylor's troops resided at Corpus Christi were also buried at the little cemetery on the bluff overlooking the encampment. If any of these graves were ever marked, however, there is no indication of it now. Following the troops' departure in March 1846, Corpus Christi residents began using the two-acre site, now called "Old Bayview Cemetery," for civilian burials. Today, it can still be found near Corpus Christi's central business district, where the site is surrounded on three sides by a chain link fence. Several grave markers seem to have been deliberately tipped over or broken, providing evidence that a lack of fencing on one side has invited vandalism. Trash and weeds further mar its appearance. A Texas State Historical Marker located near the cemetery's entrance confirms its status as the oldest U.S. military cemetery in Texas.[26]

---

[25] Henry, 37-38.

[26] Personal observation by the author, October 1993 and September 1995. NEW NOTE: During a subsequent visit in 2002, I was pleased to see that the

Port Lavaca, Texas

Approximately 80 miles north of Corpus Christi lies the city of Port Lavaca, one of the oldest coastal settlements in Texas. It was here, during the summer of 1846, that some of the volunteer regiments assigned to Gen. John E. Wool's "Army of the Center" were landed from ships or were ordered to camp *enroute* to San Antonio. Although these troops were present here only briefly, muster rolls, rosters, and the diaries and letters of soldiers confirm that several were discharged on account of illness. A lesser number died and were no doubt buried nearby.

Although the number of graves seems to be small, ascertaining their locations is complicated by the fact that there was more than one encampment in the vicinity of Port Lavaca. In his diary, Capt. Jefferson Peak of the First Regiment of Kentucky Mounted Volunteers told of being detached to go to San Antonio on September 12, 1846. When he returned to Lavaca on September 23, Peak stopped first at "Camp Calhoun." The campsite, thought the middle-aged officer, had some delightful features, particularly the sea breeze that blew from "8 oclock [sic] in the morning until 5 in the evening." In a letter to his wife, he wrote that Camp Calhoun was "a more healthful place than we have been for a long time." It was situated, he wrote, "but a few miles from the Gulf of Mexico…1 ½ miles from a beautiful Bay in the midst of a thick Grove which is just large enough to shelter the whole regiment—man and horse—from the intense heat of the sun." Despite these benefits and contrary to his assertion that it was a "healthful place," Peak also admitted that when he returned from San Antonio, he "found our redgiment [sic]…in a horrid condishion [sic] indead [sic] nearly ½ Sick and ½ of our company sick."[27]

This situation was owing, Peak surmised, to "bad" or

upkeep and appearance of the cemetery had greatly improved.
[27] Edith Rydell Roberts, ed., *The Mexican War Logbook & Letters of Captain Jefferson Peak* (Richardson, Texas: Descendants of Mexican War Veterans, 1996), 11.

"indifferent" water and "a low flat marsh land" adjacent to the camp. Five days later, he traveled "to Camp Lavaco [sic] 5 miles from the Lavaco [sic] village." Here, wrote the Kentuckian, "we had Still wors [sic] water and our Sickness increased rapidaly [sic]." In some cases, Peak confided in a letter to his wife, it "had proved fatal."[28]

A roster of the Kentucky Mounted Volunteers corroborates Peak's observations. Between September 15 and October 11, 1846, no fewer than six Kentuckians succumbed to the effects of an unspecified "fever," including a private in Peak's company, Juba M. Jones. A larger number of men were given disability discharges and sent home. Some, no doubt, died during the journey or shortly after arrival. Others, too ill to go anywhere, remained behind when the regiment moved on to San Antonio.[29]

According to Sam Chamberlain, the celebrated author of *My Confession*, the 2nd Regiment of Illinois Volunteers also suffered several losses while camped on the Texas coast. When they landed in August 1846, wrote Chamberlain, the regiment "went into Camp on a low prairie, twelve miles from La Vaca." The ground, he complained, "was covered with water" and "it seemed to rain all the time." Before long, "the measles and the Scarlet Fever broke out among the troops." Owing to "a great scarcity of doctors, hospital tents, and medical attendants," recalled the self-proclaimed rogue, "many of the men died here."[30] They don't appear to have been Illinois soldiers, however. A roster of the 2nd Illinois Volunteers lists only two fatalities at Lavaca.[31]

---

[28] Ibid.

[29] Kentucky Adjutant General, *Report of the Adjutant General of the State of Kentucky: Mexican War Veterans* (Frankfort: Capitol Office, John D. Woods, Public Printer and Binder, 1889), 2-28.

[30] Samuel E. Chamberlain, *My Confession: The Recollections of a Rogue* (New York: Harper & Brothers, Publishers, 1956), 37.

[31] Illinois Adjutant General's Office, *Record of Service of Illinois Soldiers in the Black Hawk War, 1831-1832 and in the Mexican War, 1846-1848* (Springfield, Illinois: 1887), 229-243.

San Antonio, Texas

In August and September 1846, General John E. Wool assembled his "Army of the Center," composed primarily of volunteer regiments, at San Antonio, Texas. Apart from a company of dragoon regulars stationed near Mission Concepción, most of these troops were camped at a site located about five miles north of the city's main and military plazas, where Wool probably had his headquarters. This place, where the volunteers set up their tents, was given the name "Camp Crockett," in honor of Alamo defender David Crockett.

Although a Texas Historical Commission marker at San Pedro Park identifies it as the site of Camp Crockett,[32] at least one local historian believes that Wool's troops were actually camped at what is now Brackenridge Park[33]. The Arkansas volunteers, apparently, were camped at three places. The first, recalled a former soldier several years later, was "on top of a bare rocky hill" where there was no shade from the hot Texas sun. Because that site seemed unsuitable, Colonel Yell, commanding the regiment, moved his men to "a very nice flat with shade trees, and also much nearer the water." General Wool afterward directed Yell to move his soldiers to Camp Crockett, wrote the veteran, "a dry place...three or four miles from San Antonio and no shade," where "the men fell sick and many died." Today, this description fits neither San Pedro Park or Brackenridge Park.[34]

Muster rolls confirm the man's recollections. No less than 24 Arkansas volunteers had their military service cut short by untimely deaths at San Antonio. Some died while the entire regiment was there. Others, too ill to move, were left behind when Wool's army departed San Antonio in late September.[35] As elsewhere, the location

---

[32] Personal observation by the author, October 1993.

[33] This refers to independent historian Kevin Young, now a resident of Castroville, Texas.

[34] Desmond Walls Allen, *Arkansas' Mexican War Soldiers* (Conway, Arkansas: Desmond Walls Allen, 1988), 33.

[35] Ibid., 43-133.

of the graves of these soldiers is unknown. Other regiments fared better. Only one Illinois volunteer died at Camp Crockett[36] and Capt. William's independent company of Kentucky Volunteers lost not a single man.[37]

Fort Texas, a.k.a. Fort Brown, Texas

In April 1846, shortly after the "Army of Occupation" had taken up a position on the north bank of the Rio Grande, opposite Matamoros, one of Taylor's officers was murdered by Mexican rancheros. His grave was the first of many that were dug on a flat piece of terrain that lay between the western wall of an earthen fortification originally called "Fort Texas" and the nearby Rio Grande. This "burying ground" is clearly marked on an 1847 map of the site.

More graves were added in May 1846 after Mexican forces in Matamoros began a siege and artillery bombardment of Fort Texas. When it ended six days later, the fort's defenders had suffered two fatalities: Maj. Jacob Brown, for whom the fort was afterward named, and Sgt. Horace Weigart of the Seventh Infantry. Weigart, who was killed by grapeshot on May 3, seems to have been an especially unlucky fellow. After his body was laid out in the fort's hospital tent, crowded with sick and wounded soldiers, a shell fell through the roof and exploded, decapitating his corpse. By some miracle, no one else was injured. To Lt. Napoleon Dana, it appeared as though the Mexicans had "a special spite against that particular man." That evening, after dark, Lieutenant Dana, who owed the unfortunate Weigart $255, was put in charge of his burial detail. "I took the company," he wrote to his wife Sue, "and executed the duty without even a whisper. We dug his grave in a trench at the banks of the river and laid him quietly in it and a person twenty yards off would have heard nothing of it."[38] The next day, when a Mexican artillery shell

---

[36] Illinois Adjutant General's Office, 237.
[37] Kentucky Adjutant General, 150-153.
[38] Ferrell, 59-60.

struck Weigart's grave, partly unearthing his body, Lieutenant Dana must have been convinced that the his former sergeant was truly jinxed.

Major Brown, who was severely wounded in the leg on May 6th, expired only hours before the siege was lifted on May 9th. He was afterward interred at the base of a new flagpole that had been erected inside the walls of the fort. Lt. George Stevens, a young dragoon officer who drowned in the Rio Grande on May 18, was buried beside Major Brown. An engraving depicting the interior of the fort, which appeared in Thomas B. Thorpe's *Our Army on the Rio Grande*, shows the two mounds of earth side-by-side. Two years later, the bones of Major Brown were reburied in an army cemetery established on an island in the center of a nearby lagoon or *resaca*.[39] It is uncertain whether or not the remains of Lieutenant Stevens, Sergeant Weigart, and the unknown number of others who had since been interred in the burial ground established outside the walls of the fort were also moved.

Rancho de Carricitos, Texas

On April 25, 1846, Capt. Seth Thornton, leading a scouting party upriver from Fort Texas, was ambushed at a *hacienda* called Rancho de Carricitos. Although outnumbered, the Americans fought back, losing one officer and thirteen enlisted men. After Thornton's men surrendered, two more privates died from their wounds, apparently while in captivity in Matamoros. The burial places of all sixteen are unknown, but it seems likely that the men killed in the skirmish were buried at the spot where they fell, and, in all likelihood, they remain there to this day. The soldiers who died while prisoners may either have been buried in Matamoros or their bodies returned to General Taylor's forces at Fort Texas. Unfortunately, all the official reports of

---

[39] Chula T. and Sam S. Griffin, *Records of Interments in the National Cemetery at Alexandria, Louisiana and a Brief History of Fort Brown, Texas* (Brownsville, Texas: Chula T. and Sam S. Griffin, 1987), 43-44. In 1909, Brown's remains were moved a third time, to the U.S. National Cemetery in Alexandria, Louisiana, where they repose today

this affair, which led to a U.S. declaration of war against Mexico two weeks later, are silent regarding the disposal of the remains of the soldiers who were killed and none of the literature that mentions the incident offers any clues.[40]

Palo Alto Battlefield, Texas

Three days after Thornton's command was attacked, a group of Texas Mounted Volunteers, whose commanding officer was the celebrated Capt. Samuel H. Walker, were similarly ambushed by Mexican troops midway between present-day Port Isabel and Matamoros. Walker was not present. Altogether, six men were killed. Like Thornton's soldiers, what became of the Texans' bodies is unknown. It is probable, however, that they were buried at the place where they fell by their fellow "Rangers," not far from the site of what was soon to become Palo Alto Battlefield.[41]

On May 8, 1846, General Taylor, with an army of about 2,000 men was marching from Point Isabel to relieve the defenders of Fort Texas when he found his progress blocked by Arista's army. Amazingly, during the afternoon-long battle that ensued, only five U.S. soldiers were killed. Ten, who received serious wounds, died later, some within hours of the battle. Others clung to life for days, some for several weeks. The two most celebrated of the wounded were Brevet Maj. Samuel Ringgold of the 3rd Artillery and Captain John Page of the 4th Infantry. On May 9th, all the U.S. wounded were transported back to Point Isabel[42] while the bodies of the Mexican soldiers General Arista had left behind were buried on the battlefield by the Americans. Bones bleaching in the sun months, even years, after the battle attested to the tenacity of the wounded,

---

[40] 30th Congress, 1st Session, *House Executive Document No. 60: Mexican War Correspondence* (Washington, D.C.: Wendell & Van Benthuysen, 1848), 288-292.

[41] Edward D. Mansfield, *The Mexican War* (New York: Barnes & Co., 1848), p. 34; Charles D. Spurlin, *Texas Veterans in the Mexican War* (Victoria, Texas: Charles D. Spurlin, 1984), 212-214.

[42] Henry, 93-94.

some of whom crawled off to die alone in the underbrush, apparently determined not to be taken prisoner by the *gringos*. Whether the bodies of the few U.S. soldiers who had been killed in battle were buried at Palo Alto or were taken to Point Isabel is uncertain.[43]

Point Isabel (Fort Polk), Texas

Ringgold, who was struck by Mexican grapeshot in both thighs, lingered for nearly three days. During that time he was "placed in the very best quarters that could be afforded and his wounds were dressed" by Dr. Bernard M. Byrne. "He complained but little," wrote Thomas Bangs Thorpe, "and at intervals slept." While awake, Ringgold "spoke of the incidents of the battle, and dwelt particularly on the effects of the artillery." During the early morning hours of May 11th, "death came upon him, yet he seemed unconscious of its approach, and continued to converse with his friends." "At a little past midnight," recalled Thorpe, he "resignedly breathed his last."[44]

At 3 p.m. that same day, Major Ringgold was buried with full military honors outside the earthen walls of Fort Polk, the fortified depot that General Taylor had established on the site two months earlier. Afterward, his grave seems to have become something of a tourist attraction for newly-arrived troops. On July 20, 1846, Stephen F. Nunnelee, a private of the company of "Eutaw Rangers" in the Alabama Regiment recalled in his journal a recent visit to Point Isabel. "The most interesting thing there," he wrote, "is Maj. Ringgold's grave. It is fenced in with Mexican gun barrels taken on the 8th and 9th."[45] A few days later, Pvt. Benjamin F. Scribner of the Indiana Volunteers, in the company of some friends, also visited

---

[43] Coker, 28; Ferrell, 67. Lt. Dana, who was at Fort Brown on May 8th, said the bodies of both Americans and Mexicans were buried on the battlefield but his information was second-hand. Mrs. Chapman, who visited the battlefield a few years later said she saw the bones of horses "and probably some of men" at Palo Alto.

[44] Thorpe, 117.

[45] Steven R. Butler, ed., *The Eutaw Rangers in the War with Mexico* (Richardson, Texas: Descendants of Mexican War Veterans, 1998), 82.

Point Isabel. Like Nunnelee, they stopped to see Ringgold's grave. "It is enclosed with a wooden fence," Scribner wrote, "the rails of which are filled with holes, so as to admit musket barrels." These muskets, he added, "form the palings, the bayonets serving as pickets." Ringgold's tombstone, noted the young soldier, consisted of "two boards painted black." Scribner also observed "the newly made graves of volunteers [that] were scattered around, with no names to distinguish them."[46]

Grave of Major Ringgold.

Muster rolls and rosters confirm that many of the regiments that camped near Point Isabel on their way up or down the Rio Grande left sick soldiers in the hospital at Point Isabel. When these men died, as many did, they were buried outside the walls of Fort Polk. The location of this burial ground is uncertain.

Resaca de la Palma Battlefield, Texas

The Battle of Resaca de la Palma, which immediately followed the Battle of Palo Alto, led to Taylor's defeat of General Arista and the hasty withdrawal of the Mexican army back across the Rio Grande to Matamoros. The engagement, which took place on May 9, 1846, also resulted in 33 U.S. fatalities. Eleven wounded U.S. soldiers

---

[46] Scribner, 20.

expired afterward, one as late as June 15th.[47]

On May 10th, Capt. William S. Henry of the 3rd Infantry afterward recalled, both U.S. and captured Mexican soldiers "were actively employed burying the dead." Lieutenants Zebulon M. P. Inge, Richard E, Cochrane, and Theodore L. Chadbourne, he noted, all of whom had been killed by Mexican cannon fire during a charge on horseback, "were buried with funeral honors." In contrast, wrote T. B. Thorpe, the enlisted men were interred in one common grave.[48]

"Lieutenant Inge and his fellow dragoons," recalled Thorpe, were buried "side by side" on the south side of the resaca, "a few paces from the road." Chadbourne's grave, was "slightly distinguished from those about it" and located farther along, "in an open space on the right." A primitively-sketched plan of the battleground, drawn by an anonymous artist after the fighting had stopped, indicated the spot where Cochrane was buried, as Captain Henry recalled, in an "unsodded grave by the road side, with its rude paling" marking "the spot where sleep those who died gallantly in battle." When it was published, Thorpe's book also included illustrations of the graves of the three unfortunate officers.[49]

Before the end of 1846, the remains of lieutenants Cochrane and Chadbourne were disinterred from their battlefield graves and returned to their homes, in Pennsylvania and Vermont respectively.[50] If the body of Lieutenant Inge was returned to his native Alabama, this information does not appear in any contemporary accounts of the war. It is equally uncertain whether the remains of the enlisted men whose bodies were interred at Resaca de la Palma were ever

---

[47] 29th Congress, 2nd Session. *Senate Document No. 4: Report of the Secretary of War, Showing the Names of the officers and men killed, wounded, or missing, in the battles of Palo Alto and Resaca de la Palma* (Washington: 1846), 4.

[48] Henry, p. 104; Thorpe, 113.

[49] Henry, p. 104; The Editors of American Heritage, *Texas and the War with Mexico* (New York: American Heritage Publishing Co., 1961), 77; Thorpe, 97, 100, & 103.

[50] *Niles' National Register*, Baltimore, Maryland, January 2, 1847, 274; Jim W. Corder, *Hunting Lieutenant Chadbourne* (Athens, Georgia: University of Georgia Press, 1995), 38-39.

removed to another site or if they are remain buried in their original graves, which now lie well within the city limits of Brownsville, Texas.

Graves of Lieut. Z. M. P. Inge and his dragoons.

Grave of Lieut. T. L. Chadbourne.

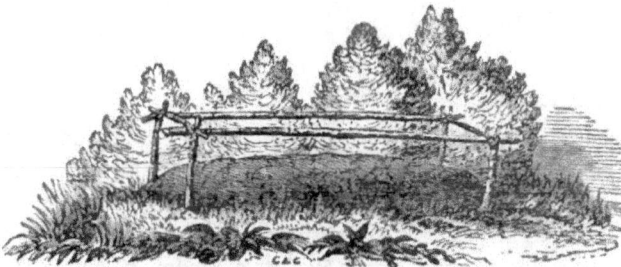

Grave of Lieut. R. E. Cochrane.

Two years after the battle, Mrs. Helen Chapman, the wife of an army officer, visited both Palo Alto and Resaca de la Palma in the company of Major John B. Scott, who had participated in the affairs of May 8 and 9, 1846. "The scene [at Resaca de la Palma] was so, so tranquil," Mrs. Chapman mused, "I could scarcely bring myself to believe it has been stained with blood." Closer inspection, however, soon showed that it had been. "As we rode down to the spot," Mrs. Chapman wrote in a letter, "all along in relief against the green grass, were the blackened bones of horses and men, fragments of shoes, of woolen cloth, of harness, of capes, fertile proofs of a deadly encounter." These, she noted, "were mostly Mexicans who fell in that line, some of whom "were buried by our soldiers and some remained where they fell."[51]

Further along, Mrs. Chapman continued, "we came to a very beautiful spot, a large green open space which was the camping ground of General Arista." On the opposite side of the road, she noted, "are two circular places where the turf has been turned up, and there lie the bodies of those who fell upon the field." It was here, she wrote, that: "Two large pits were dug and into these were thrown Americans and Mexicans." Where Arista's tent once stood, she remarked, "are three or four graves, two of Sergeants and two, I believe, of Officers whose bodies have since been removed."[52] The officers she referred to were probably Cochrane and Chadbourne, although one could have been Lt. Jacob Blake, a topographical engineer who was killed on the day of the battle by "accidental fire of his own pistol."[53]

[51] Caleb Coker, ed., *The News from Brownsville: Helen Chapman's Letters from the Texas Military Frontier, 1848-1852* (Austin: Texas State Historical Association, 1992), 28-29.
[52] Ibid.
[53] 29th Congress, 2nd Session, *House Executive Document No. 119: Message from the President of the United States...* (Washington, D.C.: Ritchie & Heiss, Printers, 1847), 121.

Lower Rio Grande Valley (Texas and Mexico)

Within days of the Battles of Palo Alto and Resaca de la Palma, volunteer organizations raised in the various states began to arrive in the Lower Rio Grande Valley. The first to reach Point Isabel, in mid-May 1846, were companies of three and six-months volunteers from Louisiana, Texas and Alabama who had rushed to respond to General Edmund Gaines' well-intentioned but illegal call-up. These were followed in June, July and August by congressionally-authorized regiments of twelve-months volunteers, full of patriotic fervor and eager to do battle with the Mexicans. However, no sooner did these troops reach the seat of war than they began to die in alarmingly large numbers and not from enemy bullets. Instead, most were the victims of illness, primarily measles and dysentery, that swept through the camps like wildfire owing to poor sanitation, overcrowding, and a lack of knowledge about how germs are spread.

During the summer of 1846, the volunteer regiments were stationed for varying lengths of time at the northern tip of Brazos Island, at Point Isabel (now Port Isabel), at the mouth of the Rio Grande, on a cactus and rattlesnake-infested ridge called Camp Belknap—a site which overlooked the nearby Rio Grande, and at Fort Brown. On the Mexican side of the river, the *Rio Bravo del Norte* as the Mexicans called it, U.S. troops were camped or quartered at the villages of Burita and Lomito, which lay midway between the mouth of the river and Matamoros.

Although several soldiers wrote about deaths that occurred on desolate, windswept Brazos Island, none identified a common burial ground or specified the location of the grave of any particular individual. One soldier, however, did describe an incident that revealed one of the problems of burying deceased soldiers at a place that was so constantly exposed to the effects of wind, rain and the ever-pounding surf of the Gulf of Mexico. "One of our officers," he wrote, "when walking along the beach the other day, unconsciously trod upon the exposed body of a man partially decayed, that two

31

weeks ago was buried in six feet in the sand."[54]

Although it is known that soldiers died and were buried at the mouth of the Rio Grande, some eight miles south of Brazos Santiago Pass, the precise location of those graves is equally unknown. On August 16, 1846, Capt. Franklin Smith, of the First Regiment of Mississippi Volunteers wrote in his journal that when he first arrived at the mouth of the river, he heard guns firing. When Smith was asked by a regimental surgeon if he knew what was going on, the newly-arrived officer replied that he didn't. "He informed me that they were burying a man." Smith recalled, adding only that the unfortunate soldier's name was "T. W. Ellis of the Yazoo volunteers...a bright eyed fine looking fellow who lived a short time ago at Camden, Marion County."[55]

The site of Camp Belknap, a long, low hillock overlooking the Rio Grande, crowned by mesquite trees and all manner of prickly, thorny plants, has probably changed very little in appearance during the more than one-hundred and fifty years that have passed since thousands of volunteers were stationed there during the summer of 1846. Although most men seem to have preferred it to windswept Brazos Island, with its flies and constantly blowing sand, Camp Belknap was nonetheless an unhealthy spot where a significantly large number of soldiers succumbed to a variety of illnesses, including mumps, measles, and dysentery. Pvt. Thomas Tennery of the Fourth Regiment of Illinois Volunteers was one of a number of soldiers who felt compelled to record the deaths of their comrades in journals and letters. All, however, were generally vague in their descriptions of burial sites. On August 25, 1846, Tennery wrote about the death and funeral of one man, whose final resting place could have been almost anywhere:

Jerry McPherson of this company died last night. He was a fine young man, who left his home in as fine spirits as anyone. But alas

---

[54] Scribner, 19-20.
[55] Chance, *Franklin Smith*, 8.

we have to leave him beneath the sandy turf of the chaparral grove. By him lie some of the Kentucky troops. There are interred in this vicinity a great many men from the states and a funeral or two takes place every day.[56]

During his regiment's sojourn at Camp Belknap, Private Tennery recorded the death and burial of several other Illinois men who were laid "in the vault without coffin or box, for the boards or plank cannot be found in this place" but his descriptions of the places where they were interred never improved. One man, he noted simply, "lies beneath this chaparral grove, with prickly pears growing above his grave."[57] Other writers were equally vague. Capt. Sydenham Moore, commanding a company of Alabama volunteers, wrote in his journal that he was "growing sick & tired of hearing so often the dead march following to the grave some of our brave volunteers" but added only that "they sleep under the branches of the wild muskeet trees."[58]

In 1970 archaeologist Elton Prewitt discovered a burial ground containing the remains of soldiers who died during the U.S.-Mexican War in the vicinity of Camp Belknap. The site has since been registered with the Texas Historical Commission. It is located on the *Loma de los Ebonitos*, a small hillock situated on the north side of the Boca Chica Road (State Highway 14), directly across from a Texas Historical Commission roadside marker that was erected in 1996 to commemorate Camp Belknap.[59] Whether this spot was the only burial site in the vicinity or if there were others is uncertain. However, given that the ridge upon which the encampment was located is approximately two miles in length and that the several regiments who erected their tents here seem to have been spread out

---

[56] Livingston-Little, 16-17.

[57] Ibid., 18.

[58] Butler, *Eutaw Rangers*, 21.

[59] Rachel Feit, Helen Simons, and Mike Davis, *Texas Military Sites: A Guide to Materials in the Holdings of the Office of the State Archeologist, Texas Historical Commission* (Austin: Texas Historical Commission, 1996), 8; on-site observation by the author, May & October 1993 and May 1997.

along its entire length, it seems likely that the *Loma de los Ebonitos* cemetery is but one among several burial grounds that accommodated the soldiers who died at Camp Belknap.

The smaller number of soldiers who died while camped near the villages of Burita and Lomito, on the Mexican side of the Rio Grande between its mouth and Matamoros, were no doubt buried in the vicinity of those places but as with Camp Belknap, the location of their graves are uncertain. One soldier, who was stationed at Burita early in the war, recalled the funeral of a member of the Louisiana Volunteers, who died there. His words also say a lot about the attitude some soldiers had about the type of death that most Mexican War soldiers suffered:

> There were no boards to make a coffin and so they wrapped his blanket around him, and carrying him to a bier, they marched to a high piece of ground, where his grave had been dug, and after firing a volley over him, a rude cross was placed in the earth to mark the spot. Many were heard to exclaim: "It is a pity that he had not fallen on the battle-field." And yet it is hard to say whether the poor fellow would have gained more glory. A soldier enlists for the chances of death, though few who do so think of it at the time. And yet just as much honour, gratitude, and respect is due, whether he falls on the battle-field or not, so long as he dies in the service of his country.[60]

Matamoros, Tamulipas

Matamoros, now one of the largest cities in Northern Mexico, was abandoned by General Arista's forces within days of their defeat at Resaca de la Palma. Shortly afterward, the town was taken by U.S. troops without firing a shot. Almost immediately, an army hospital was established in a public building located on the city's main plaza. Here, soldiers too sick to accompany their regiments to Camargo or other places, along with those who became ill while on garrison duty, were taken for treatment. Most of these, it appears, were discharged on a surgeon's certificate of disability and sent home. Many others

---

[60] Samuel C. Reid, Jr., *The Scouting Expeditions of McCulloch's Texas Rangers* (Philadelphia: G. B. Zieber and Co., 1847), 20.

died. The number who recovered is unknown. Interestingly, although Camargo is often portrayed by historians as the deadliest encampment in Northern Mexico, in terms of deaths from sickness, it may be that Matamoros is more deserving of that distinction. A random examination of the rosters of regiments that were active in Northern Mexico in 1846 and 1847 reveals that in many cases, more men died at Matamoros than Camargo. The 3rd Regiment of Illinois Volunteers, for example, lost 23 men at Camargo during its twelve months' service. During the same period, 43 members of the regiment, or nearly twice as many, died at Matamoros. The 4th Illinois regiment fared similarly, losing 34 men at Matamoros compared to 25 at Camargo.

Col. Samuel Ryan Curtis of the 3rd Regiment of Ohio Volunteers, previously mentioned, commanded the Matamoros garrison for several months in 1846 and 1847. During that time, he kept a journal in which he drew a map of the city, marking on it the location of American graves.

"The large grave yard on the S.W.," wrote Curtis, "adjoining the enclosed grave yard of the Mexicans; is the general deposit where all our soldiers who die in the hospitals have been placed. The other two little graveyards are those of the 3rd Regiment [of Ohio Volunteers]. One of the latter, he noted, "is north of our encampment by a tree standing lonely on the plain."[61]

The large grave yard mentioned by Curtis still exists and has been visited by this writer. There is, however, no trace of the American burial ground adjacent to it. From all appearances, city streets and buildings now cover the site. By the same token, the smaller burial grounds identified by Curtis, which lay beside the river, seem also to have been covered by pavement.[62]

Reynosa, Tamaulipas and Mier, Nuevo Leon

In their diaries, letters, and recollections, U.S. soldiers who wrote

---

[61] Chance, *Mexico Under Fire*, 25, 45 and 48.
[62] Personal observation by the author during a visit to Matamoros in 1993.

about the towns of Reynosa or Mier, both of which are located on the Rio Grande, have left posterity with little information regarding the death and burial of American soldiers at those two places. Although there are most certainly some U.S. graves at both, the number is probably very small, in comparison to other Mexican towns that were garrisoned by U.S. forces.

Camargo, Tamulipas

One place in Northern Mexico where there are undoubtedly hundreds, perhaps thousands, of graves of U.S. soldiers is Camargo, located on the east side or right bank of the Rio San Juan, a few miles below the point where it empties into the Rio Grande.

It was to Camargo, about 130 miles upriver from the mouth of the Rio Grande, that Gen. Zachary Taylor moved most of his troops during the late summer of 1846, in preparation for his advance on Monterey. When the army departed, however, Taylor left some regiments behind to garrison the town. Two of these were the Regiment of Tennessee Mounted Volunteers, who had an unusually high number of men on the sick rolls, and the First Regiment of Alabama Volunteers, who were assigned the unenviable task of taking care of the ill Tennesseans. Some Kentuckians also stayed behind, along with a large number of Mississippians who were "left sick in their tents unprovided for," wrote an Alabama volunteer in his journal.[63]

Although most of his regiment went forward with Taylor, Capt. Franklin Smith of the Mississippi Volunteers was ordered to stay behind to assist the regular quartermaster, Col. George H. Crosman. In his capacity as an assistant quartermaster, it was Captain Smith's job to organize supply trains that departed Camargo for Monterey and other places further south.

During the time he was stationed at Camargo, the Mississippian kept a journal, in which he recorded his thoughts and impressions of the town, which soon became notorious as a "yawning graveyard" on

---

[63] Butler, *The Eutaw Rangers in the War with Mexico*, 87.

account of the deaths that occurred there at the rate of a half-dozen per day. The demand for coffins was so great, wrote Smith, that by September 9th, "all the lumber gave out and Capt. Crosman told the applicants that they would have to give their friends a soldier's burial—i.e. bury them in their blankets without coffins." In time, the sorrowful officer added, other formalities ceased to be observed. "Hundreds of America's noble and generous sons," he remarked, "sleep in this soil without having received the rites of the decencies of Scriptures."[64]

The large number of deaths obviously disturbed the sensitive and insightful Smith who, from time to time, poured out his emotions in his journal entries. On November 15, 1846, a Sunday, he wrote:

> Platoon after platoon is firing around me every day from every point the soldiers are dying—But who thinks of a private a volunteer private? He dies and is buried uncoffined! The only announcement not of his death but that one of the genus homo is dead is the firing of a half dozen guns—the shooters trying to fire together and trying at nothing else and thinking of nothing else—The firing announces that homo is dead—Black Thompson Smith Jones Clay Polk Mason Brown Peterson whatever his name or lineage it boots not to say nor is it said or known but to the man detailed to given him rice water and close his eyes—Barem go the guns—homo is dead! That is all that is known to the surrounding thousands.[65]

Smith was not the only one to notice that the death of a soldier had become so routine that other men paid little attention. In his journal, Pvt. Stephen Nunnelee, recalled a member of the Kentucky regiment who had died:

> One of the men who was detailed to dig his grave, passed by his Captain's tent, paying particular attention to a large piece of pork, and some hard crackers, which he had in his hand." Wher'er you going Bill?" "Going to dig Jess Chamber's grave," Replied "Bill." "The Hell!" exclaimed the Captain. "Is Jess dead?" "Yes," replied

---

[64] Smith, *The Mexican War Journal of Captain Franklin Smith*, 21 & 63.
[65] Ibid, 111.

Bill, not forgetting his meat and bread. How perfectly indifferent a man can become. He soon loses all of those finer and sympathetic feelings that ennobles his nature. And this is pretty much the case with all.[66]

Earlier in the war, another soldier recalled the first time he and his comrades had seen a man die and how he had been struck by the callousness of one of the regulars who told them: "You will all d—n soon get used to such scenes." Intending perhaps to shock the "green" soldiers, the man added that "after the battle of the 9th, we had been hard at work burying the dead, when coming across a fellow that had on a better pair of boots than I had, we exchanged; and after drinking the contents of his canteen, I made a pillow of the corpse, and never slept sounder in my life."[67]

Despite the frequency with which it occurred, some men never grew accustomed to seeing their fellow soldiers die. On one occasion a Texas volunteer, one of a breed of men noted for their seeming indifference to hardship and suffering, betrayed his true feelings when he wrote of visiting the hospital at Camargo where he witnessed the "most painful of all scenes...a young soldier in the bloom and hey-day of life...lying on the couch of death, with no kind friend or relative near to speak a soothing word of consolation, or to remember him to those he loved, or bear to them his dying wish, as his last breath vanishes upon the atmosphere of a foreign land, and sinking into the arms of death, not even to be mentioned or remembered for the service he had rendered, or known to the world as one who had fought in the defence of his country's cause."[68]

Later, when the same man saw another soldier "carried out to be buried, who had fought bravely at the late battles," he could not help but think how sad it was that the "poor fellow...was now to be entombed without a tear, or hardly a regret, to follow him to his

[66] Butler, *The Eutaw Rangers in the War with Mexico*, 89.
[67] Samuel C. Reid, Jr., *The Scouting Expeditions of McCulloch's Texas Rangers* (Philadelphia: G. B. Zieber and Co., 1847), 19.
[68] Reid, 75.

grave, save that which the volley of muskets echoed as the fresh green earth was piled over his corpse."[69]

Most of the Americans who died at Camargo were undoubtedly buried on the left or west bank of the Rio San Juan, where the soldiers' camps were situated. A smaller number may be buried on the other side of the river. After the passage of more than one-hundred and fifty years, however, the exact location of any of the army's burial sites are now uncertain. Although a precise number is not available, it is possible that before the war was over, that between 2,000 and 3,000 U.S. soldiers died and were buried at Camargo, which would make it the site of the largest concentration of American graves in Mexico.

Monterey, Nuevo Leon

The city of Monterey (now spelled *Monterrey*), Nuevo Leon was occupied nearly the entire length of the U.S.-Mexican War. In addition to any deaths from disease and accidents that occurred there among troops who formed the city's garrison, the battle that was fought at Monterey in September 1846 resulted in 146 U.S. fatalities.

While stationed at Monterey, reported Capt. William S. Henry, the 3rd Infantry Regiment constructed a cemetery where initially, only officers who were killed in battle were buried. Henry's book, *Campaign Sketches of the War with Mexico*, included a picture of the burial ground, with a description of the site and the services that were held there:

> It is a square inclosure, situated a few yards to the west of the road leading to Monterey, and directly in front of the camp of the regiment. The wall is four feet high, and on the face toward the camp there is a rectangular pillar surmounted by a cross. It is built of blocks of white limestone neatly dressed. The remains of the officers having been disinterred from the shallow graves in which they had been placed on the battle-field, at 4 P.M. on the 25th of November the funeral ceremony of the gallant dead took place. The 4th Infantry

---

[69] Ibid.

were the escort, and the 3d attended as mourners. It was a sad and melancholy duty, yet one which carried some little consolation to the officers of the regiment, and will be of inestimable satisfaction to their friends and relatives. The service for the dead was read by Major L. Thomas. There they lie, sleeping as they fought, side by side; and there they should be permitted to remain, surrounded by towering mountains, and in the midst of scenery unsurpassed for grandeur and beauty, until the 'last trump' shall summon them before their Maker.[70]

Cemetery of the 3d Infantry.

Henry also recorded the names of the officers who were first interred in the cemetery: Maj. Lewis N. Morris; Capt. George P. Field; Maj. Philip N. Barbour; Lt. Douglass S. Irwin; Lt. Robert Hazlitt; and Maj. William W. Lear, the only one of the six who lived for any length of time following the battle. Lear lingered for more than a month after being severely wounded while "gallantly leading his regiment in the storming of Monterey," dying at the end of October.[71]

Officers who were later laid to rest in the 3rd Infantry Cemetery at Monterey. Included Brigadier-General Thomas L. Hamer of the

---

[70] Henry, 250.
[71] Ibid.

Volunteers, who passed away on December 2, 1846, and lieutenants Charles Hoskins of the 4th Infantry and Lt. James S. Woods of the 2nd Infantry, both of whom had been killed in battle on September 21st.[72]

On December 3, 1846, the day before General Hamer's funeral, Capt. Franklin Smith of the Mississippi Volunteers, along with a fellow officer, rode over the battlefield where most of the soldiers had been buried. Smith had not taken part in the fighting, having been stationed at Camargo at the time of the battle. The unnamed officer showed Smith "the fort the Mississippians captured," the place where Colonel Watson of the Maryland and D.C. Volunteers had been killed and where he was buried, and where the fallen Ohio, Kentucky, and Tennessee volunteers were interred. It was not a pleasant sight. "As we rode over the ground," the Mississippian recorded later in his journal, "we saw several soldiers half out of the graves." Some were completely out. "My companion thought this done by the Mexicans," wrote Smith, "I believe it was done by wild beasts." Smith was correct, apparently. Another soldier, Texas volunteer Buck Barry, remembered that after the fighting was over, starving dogs roamed over the battlefield "eating on the carcasses of the men" who were either "overlooked or buried in shallow graves."[73]

On the evening before the 3rd Infantry Regiment was due to depart Monterey, Captain Henry visited the cemetery one last time to watch the sunset over Saddle Mountain and to bid farewell to "the graves of my brother officers." "Thank God!" he wrote, "the cross protects your precious remains from desecration." Captain Henry's faith, as it turned out, was not matched by reality. In less than thirty years, nearly every trace of the little grave-yard would be obliterated from the face of the earth.

---

[72] Ibid, 253.

[73] Chance, *The Mexican War Journal of Captain Franklin Smith*, 127; James K. Greer, *A Texas Ranger and Frontiersman: The Days of Buck Barry in Texas, 1848-1906* (Dallas, Texas: The Southwest Press, 1932), 40.

Buena Vista and Saltillo, Coahuila

The Battle of Buena Vista, which took place near Saltillo on February 22 and 23, 1847, was the bloodiest military engagement of the war, producing 267 U.S. fatalities. Out of the 456 Americans who were injured, no fewer than 25 received wounds that afterward proved mortal.[74] On the morning of February 24th, after learning that Santa Anna's army had retreated, leaving the U.S. Army in possession of the battlefield, wrote an officer of the 1st Regiment of Illinois Volunteers, "we collected and buried our dead." In his journal, Pvt. Charles Scribner of the 2nd Regiment of Indiana Volunteers recorded a much more detailed account. "Parties were sent out in all directions for the killed and wounded," wrote the young volunteer, who, along with some other Indiana soldiers, managed to secure a wagon and "went in search of others belonging to our regiment." Two of their fallen comrades, recalled the young soldier, had been stripped of their clothing, by Mexican soldiers they assumed. As Scribner and his friends lifted the corpses from the ground, he was struck by "the icy coldness of their naked bodies" which "sent a thrill of horror at every touch throughout my whole frame."[75]

The Indiana men spent the entire day "wandering over the bloody field, and burying the dead," who, prior to interment, were laid out on the ground by regiment. "Our boys were placed side by side," noted Scribner, who helped his comrades take "a lock of each one's hair, as a memento for their friends." After the graves had been filled in, he wrote, "we fixed a cross made with staves, with their names cut thereon, and raised over them a pile of stones." Before returning to camp "with a heavy heart," he concluded, "we fired three salutes" over their graves.[76]

---

[74] *Niles' National Register*, Baltimore, Maryland, January 15, 1848, 312; James Henry Carleton, *The Battle of Buena Vista, with the operations of the "Army of occupation" for one month* (New York: Harper & Bros., 1848) 190; *Executive Document No. 8*, 100-131.

[75] Benjamin F. Scribner, *Camp Life of a Volunteer* (Philadelphia: Grigg, Elliot and Co., 1847), 68.

[76] Ibid.

That evening, after supper, Scribner and his comrades buried yet another member of the Indiana regiment, who had apparently been killed by Mexican lancers while attempting "to quench his thirst and bathe his wound" in a nearby stream. "We buried him by moonlight," recalled Scribner, "on a grassy ridge near the spot where he fell."[77]

While the dead were being buried on the battlefield, Enoch C. Marsh, a civilian teamster from Illinois, organized a wagon train to transport the wounded of both sides to Saltillo, seven miles to the north.[78] The bodies of some fallen U.S. officers were taken there also. Santiago Cathedral, a grand edifice facing Saltillo's main plaza, was quickly converted into a hospital for the wounded. In the meantime, the dead officers were carried to a hillside overlooking the city, where an artillery redoubt equipped with two 24-pounder cannons and commanded by Brevet Maj. Lucien B. Webster had been established prior to the battle. Its original purpose had been to counter any Mexican attempt to retake Saltillo; now it served to defend the dead, if necessary, from grave-looters, one of the reasons the site was chosen.[79] Among those participating in the burial of the American officers was John Gregg, the noted frontier scholar. Gregg, who had accompanied General Wool's "Army of the Center" when it marched out of San Antonio, Texas in late September 1846, had attached himself to the 1st Regiment of Arkansas Volunteers. In a letter to the *Arkansas Intelligencer*, dated March 22, 1847, he reported the death and burial of the regiment's colonel, former Arkansas Governor Archibald Yell, who had been killed at Buena Vista:

> I informed you in my other letter of the death of Colonel Yell. Supposing his family might hereafter wish to remove his remains, we had a tin coffin prepared, which was placed in strong wooden one. The burial I superintended myself. I had him interred above the southern border of the city, at the foot of the hill, under Captain

---

[77] Ibid.

[78] Joseph E. Chance, *Jefferson Davis's Mexican War Regiment* (Jackson: University Press of Mississippi, 1991), 110.

[79] David Lavender, *Climax at Buena Vista* (Philadelphia & New York: J. B. Lippincott Co., 1966), 175.

Webster's fort, so that his grave remains protected; otherwise, there would have been much danger that Mexican rogues might have disinterred him for his burial clothes. I set a cross at his head with his name cut upon it, so that his friends may know his grave. By him, I had buried John Pelman [a private in the Arkansas regiment], with his grave marked in the same way. Near by were also buried Col. [John J.] Hardin [of the 1st Illinois Volunteers], Captain [George] Lincoln [of the 8th Infantry], Captain [Andrew R.] Porter [of the Arkansas Mounted Volunteers], and others.[80]

Among the "others" Gregg failed to name were Col. William R. McKee of the 2nd Regiment of Kentucky Foot Volunteers and his second-in-command, Lt. Col. Henry Clay, Jr.. Both McKee and Clay, son of prominent Kentucky Senator Henry Clay, had been killed in action on February 23rd. After their graves had been marked with wooden crosses, an anonymous daguerreotypist made two photographs of the Kentuckians' burial site. Each daguerreotype (now owned by the Amon Carter Museum, Fort Worth, Texas) clearly shows three freshly-dug mounds of earth (the identity of the occupant of the third grave is uncertain) surrounded by a cluster of short, leafless mesquite trees, the trunks of which seem to have been bent by the wind. What appear to be the bell towers of one or two churches can be seen below and in the distance, confirming that the site was situated on a hill overlooking the city.[81]

Tampico, Tamulipas

Following the United States Navy's seizure of the Mexican port city of Tampico in November 1846, U.S. troops were sent to guard the city. Among the soldiers whose regiments were afterward camped on the outskirts of Tampico was Private Thomas D. Tennery of the 4th Regiment of Illinois Volunteers. In his journal Tennery wrote

---

[80] Maurice Garland Fulton, ed., *Diary & Letters of Josiah Gregg*, volume 2 (Norman, Oklahoma: University of Oklahoma Press, 1941), 65; *Executive Document No. 8*, 100-130.

[81] Martha A. Sandweiss, Rick Stewart, and Ben W. Huseman, *Eyewitness to War: Prints and Daguerreotypes of the Mexican War, 1846-1848* (Fort Worth, Texas: Amon Carter Museum, 1989), 198-200.

that the Illinois men were camped "in an old field on the right of the road" just outside the city. During their stay, which lasted from late January to early March 1847 he recorded the deaths of seven soldiers. Four of these were men of his own regiment, two belonged to the 3rd Regiment of Illinois Volunteers, and one he described only as "a cavalryman." Five of the deceased soldiers, wrote Tennery, were left to "lie mouldering in their mother earth at this encampment." A sixth, Capt. Achilles Morris, was interred somewhere in the city. The unnamed cavalryman, Tennery recorded, was buried by his own comrades beside Fort Andonega, an old Mexican fortification that overlooked and guarded the mouth of the Rio Panuco near Tampico.[82]

During this same period a regiment of Tennessee volunteers was camped near Fort Andonega. One of their number, Pvt. George Thurber, later authored a book that told of his experiences during the war. One of the many illustrations that accompanied Thurber's recollections depicted the old Spanish fort, beyond which lay the encampment of the Tennesseans. In the accompanying text, Thurber identified the place that his regiment used as a burial ground: "Over the broken wall in front, you observe a hill covered with bushes— that hill is the final resting place of many soldiers of our own and of the other regiments of our brigade. The graves are on that part of it seen beyond the corner of the house."[83]

Doubtless, the several other regiments that were stationed in the vicinity of Tampico during the early months of 1847 also buried their dead at or near their respective campsites, in places that might be impossible to locate today.

Following the city's occupation by U.S. forces, there was also an army hospital established at Tampico which Furber identified as being in a large building behind a church or cathedral located on the

---

[82] D. E. Livingston-Little, ed., *The Mexican War Diary of Thomas D. Tennery* (Norman, Oklahoma: University of Oklahoma Press, 1970), 65-69.
[83] George W. Furber, *The Twelve Months Volunteer* (Cincinnati: J. A. & U. P. James, 1849), 401.

plaza. The structure had previously been used, said the soldier, as a place of "public instruction," meaning perhaps, that it had been a school.[84] Neither Furber nor any other American soldier who passed through Tampico, however, left any clues pointing to the location of the burial ground that was surely used by hospital attendants for the interment of the many soldiers who died at Tampico.

When Gen. Winfield Scott launched his invasion of Central Mexico in March 1847, most of the first troops who had garrisoned the town departed Tampico, leaving it in the hands of the Battalion of Maryland and District of Columbia Volunteers until May 1847. The Marylanders seem to have been an exceptionally healthy group. In the interval between the departure of the other regiments and their own leaving, only a single man, a private named John S. Walker, died of illness.[85] Afterward, the town was guarded by the 1st Regiment of Louisiana Volunteers, Anderson's Battalion of Mississippi Rifles, and a battalion formed of five companies of the 6th Regiment of Illinois Volunteers (also known as the 2nd Regiment of Illinois Volunteers for the War). The last-named organization suffered badly, losing no less than 78 men at Tampico.[86]

The names of several deceased Illinois soldiers appeared in the February 28, 1848 edition of the New Orleans *Picayune*, which published a roster of all those who died or were discharged from the hospital at Tampico during the months of November and December 1847 and January 1848. The paper also carried a report prepared by Assistant Surgeon Charles M. Hitchcock, who was in charge of the facility. During the last four months of 1847, wrote Hitchcock, 398 cases were treated, of which 143 died. Many, he noted, were "brought into hospital in dying condition" and most, he added, were victims of

---

[84] Ibid, 413.
[85] Charles G. Wells, *Maryland and District of Columbia Volunteers in the Mexican War* (Westminster, Maryland: Family Line Publications, 1991), 72.
[86] Illinois Adjutant General's Office, *Record of Service of Illinois Soldiers in the Black Hawk War, 1831-1832 and in the Mexican War, 1846-1848* (Springfield, Illinois: 1887), 244-265.

yellow fever. [87]

The actual number of U.S. soldiers who died and are still buried at Tampico is uncertain but a reasonable estimate, based on an average of 35 deaths per month for the approximately 19 months the city was occupied, is between 650 and 700.

During the siege and bombardment of Vera Cruz, which marked the beginning of the U.S. Army's invasion of Mexico under Gen. Winfield Scott, 9 U.S. soldiers were killed by enemy fire and 3 died of wounds, for a total of 12 fatalities. There seems to be no record of where these men were buried.

NEW MEXICO AND CALIFORNIA

The western campaign, for certain reasons, produced far fewer casualties than elsewhere. For a start, the region in which in this portion of the war was waged was sparsely populated. Owing to a complete lack of opposition, at least initially, both New Mexico and California were seized by U.S. forces without firing a shot. Later, when opposition did arise, the troops that Americans had to fight were usually not battle-hardened Mexican regulars but hastily organized local militias, or in the case of New Mexico, a band of insurrectionists seemingly loosely organized. The only exception was the Battle of El Brazito, fought on Christmas Day 1846 near present-day Las Cruces, New Mexico, between a regiment of Missouri Mounted Volunteers under Colonel Doniphan and Mexican regulars stationed at El Paso del Norte (present-day Ciudad Juarez).

New Mexico

In New Mexico, as elsewhere, the majority of deaths among U.S. troops were caused by illness. During the uprising of January and February 1847, New Mexican insurrectionists killed 25 civilians, including Governor Bent, but only 11 U.S. military personnel. In other minor actions that occurred throughout 1847, only 9 more U.S.

---

[87] *Picayune*, New Orleans, Louisiana, February 28, 1848, 33.

soldiers lost their lives during engagements with the enemy.[88]

One of the men who performed military service in New Mexico during the war was George Rutledge Gibson, a lieutenant in the Battalion of Missouri Mounted Volunteers. In a journal that he kept, Gibson identified a burial ground at Fort Marcy, an earthen fortification on a hill overlooking Santa Fe, as the final resting place of some of those who were killed, as well as soldiers who died of illness. Here is his entry for May 5, 1847:

> I visited the Fort and was not only astonished but grieved at its [the post cemetery's] magnitude. 300 new made graves attest to the mortality which existed among the troops and teamsters and three little hillocks on the side of the hill mark the spot where Gov. [Charles] Bent, Capt. [John H. K.] Burgwin, and A[lbert] G. Wilson repose. It is a melancholy spectacle to visit the ground and [it] is already an extensive Grave Yard. Various causes brought the men to an untimely end. Some from dissipation. Some from Exposure. Some the want of attention. Some broken down constitutions. Some from fever and some from the effects of colds. The health of the army here though I found good at this time, the weak and sickly having pretty much all died off. Measles was also a fruitful disease in filling up the ground.[89]

A plan of Santa Fe, drawn by Lt. J. F. Gilmore of the Army Corps of Engineers, shows the position of Fort Marcy on the heights. Nearby, separated by a road, is a cemetery. Is this the post cemetery described by Gibson? The cemetery can likewise be seen on a map published in J. T. Hughes' book, *The Doniphan Expedition*.[90]

---

[88] 30th Congress, 2nd Session, *House Executive Document No. 1: Message from the President of the United States* (Washington, D.C.: Wendell & Van Benthuysen, 1848), 520, 528-530; Ralph E. Twitchell, *Old Santa Fe* (Santa Fe: R. E. Twitchell, 1925), 124-132, 136-138, 145-146.

[89] Robert W. Frazer, ed., *Over the Chihuahua and Santa Fe Trails, 1847-1848: George Rutledge Gibson's Journal* (Albuquerque: University of New Mexico Press, 1981), 39.

[90] *Plan of Santa Fé, New Mexico*, surveyed and drawn by J. F. Gilmore, 1st Lt., U.S. Corps of Engineers, 1846-1847; . J. T. Hughes, *Doniphan's Expedition* (Cincinnati: U.P. James, 1847), 37

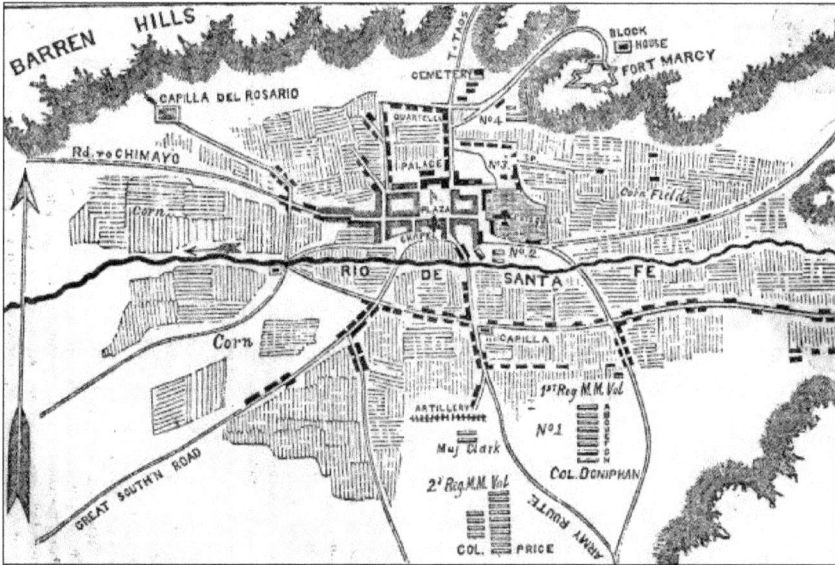

A national cemetery, located 10 blocks northwest of the city's main plaza, was later established at Santa Fe. The remains of Governor Bent were afterward moved from the post cemetery at Fort Marcy to this site and a large white marble stone was erected to mark his grave.[91] Whether the remains of any other casualties of the U.S.-Mexican War were also moved to this new cemetery is unknown.

California

As in New Mexico, battle casualties in California were light. The so-called "battles" of Dominguez Rancho (also called the "Battle of the Old Lady's Gun") and Natividad, in October and November 1847, produced only eight American fatalities between them. During the affair at San Pasqual, which was fought on December 6, 1846 between General Kearny's dragoons and a band of Californian lancers, 18 Americans were killed and a nineteenth died soon after. In the two battles that were necessary to re-take Los Angeles in January

---

[91] Mark Simmons, *Following the Santa Fe Trail: A Guide for Modern Travelers* (Santa Fe: Ancient City Press, 1986), 195.

1847, the combined forces of Commodore Stockton and General Kearny lost but a single man to enemy fire. Some lesser engagements resulted in no American fatalities at all.[92]

The four crewmembers of the *U.S.S. Savannah*, who were killed at Dominguez Rancho trying unsuccessfully to re-take Los Angeles after American forces had been driven from the city, were buried October 10, 1846 on a small island near the mouth of San Pedro Bay that the men who composed the burial detail afterward referred to as "Dead Man's Island." A fifth man, a marine named William H. Berry, was interred there the following day after he succumbed to the effects of wounds received in battle. On October 22, another seaman died of illness and was interred with the others. A sailor killed in an accident prior to the battle is also said to have been buried there. "Dead Man's Island," apparently, was an area landmark for many years, but it no longer exists. In modern times, it was completely obliterated as a result of harbor construction.[93]

Eighteen of the men who were killed or mortally wounded at San Pasqual were originally interred at the site. At first, their comrades were loath to leave them there, fearing that their graves might be robbed or dug up by the wolves that were seen lurking in the area, attracted, so one man thought, by the smell of spilt blood. In the end, it was a lack of sufficient mules to carry both the wounded and the dead that decided the matter. Under cover of darkness on December 6, 1846, the dead were buried.[94] Capt. Henry Smith Turner, in a letter to his wife that he wrote only two weeks after the incident, tells how this was done:

---

[92] J. M. Gunn, *Historical & Biographical Record of Southern California* (Chicago: Chapman Publishing Co. 1902), pp. 102-103; Edwin Bryant, *What I Saw in California* (New York: D. Appleton & Co., 1848) 397; 30th Congress, 2nd Session, *Executive Document No. 7: Notes of a Military Reconnoissance* (Washington, D. C.: Wendell & Van Benthuysen, 1848), 108-111.

[93] Mildred Brooke Hoover, Hero Eugene Rensch, Ethel Grace Rensch, and William N. Abeloe, *Historic Spots in California* (Stanford, California: Stanford University Press, 1983), 150; J. M. Gunn, 102-103.

[94] *Executive Document No. 7*, 108-109.

Then came the painful task of collecting our dead and wounded, 18 of the former, among them Capt. Johnston and Lt. Hammond (Lt. H. survived a few hours,) and 14 or 15 wounded, among them Gen. Kearny and Lt. Warner quite badly, myself very slightly. Capt. Moore and Lt. Hammond being killed the command of the Dragoons devolved upon me, and the duty of disposing of the dead and providing for the wounded had to be performed and I am unable to describe to you what were my sensations as I superintended the arrangements for the burial of the poor fellows, who but a few hours before had been in our midst without a presentiment of what so soon was to be their fate. A large grave was dug and all deposited in it, officers and men together there to remain until an opportunity is presented of paying them proper funeral honors.[95]

On December 9, Kearny's dragoons were camped on an elevated site now called "Mule Hill" when they were besieged by the Californians for a second time. Although they were able to fight them off without any further loss of life, it was here that "the brave Sergeant Cox" died of the wounds he had received on December 6. To prevent wolves from uncovering the grave and "tearing him up," he was buried "deep in the ground and covered with heavy stones."[96]

In 1846 and 1847, a regiment of New York volunteers and a battalion of Mormon volunteers performed garrison duty in both upper and lower California. It appears that the losses or both organizations were light. Where the graves of these soldiers are located is unknown.

CENTRAL MEXICO

Vera Cruz, Vera Cruz

During the siege and artillery bombardment of Vera Cruz, which marked the beginning of the U.S. Army's invasion of Mexico under

---

[95] Henry Smith Turner, *The Original Journals of Henry Smith Turner with Stephen Watts Kearny to New Mexico and California, 1846-1847* (Norman: University of Oklahoma Press, 1966), 146.

[96] 30th Congress, 2nd Session, *Executive Document No. 7*, 111.

Gen. Winfield Scott, 9 U.S. soldiers were killed by enemy fire and 3 died of wounds, for a total of 12 fatalities.[97] There seems to be no record of where these men were buried.

On April 7, 1847, shortly after the capitulation of Vera Cruz, a general hospital was established by army surgeon John B. Porter in the Franciscan convent of San Carlos, located near the city gate that led to the *mole*, or docks of the city. "The building," wrote Louis C. Duncan, a Spanish-American War veteran who drew upon the records of Major Porter to author a study of the army medical corps during the earlier Mexican conflict, "consisted of a very large church, a smaller chapel, and numerous upper rooms around the convent patio." It was, wrote Duncan, "a convenient pile of buildings, facing the sea, well-ventilated, and having a good water supply." Notwithstanding these advantages, remarked Duncan, "it was hospital in name only" that provided little but "shelter for the sick."[98]

In addition to troops who formed the city's garrison, many U.S. soldiers attached to regiments that passed through Vera Cruz on their way to Puebla, Mexico City and other points inland, were taken ill and hospitalized at the old convent. The precise number who died is unknown but the February 21, 1848 issue of the New Orleans *Picayune* listed no less than 7 deaths at the hospital in Vera Cruz for the period January 18-26, 1848,[99] an average of one per day. A later edition of the newspaper reported that for the period April 1-15, 1848, there were 23 deaths at Vera Cruz,[100] resulting in a slightly higher average of approximately 1.5 deaths per day. If these averages held steady for the entire period that the hospital was in operation, it is probable that from 480 to 720 U.S. soldiers died at Vera Cruz between April 1847 and early August 1848, when the last U.S. troops departed the city.

---

[97] *Niles'*, January 15, 1848, 312.

[98] Louis C. Duncan, "A Medical History of General Zachary Taylor's Army of Occupation in Texas and Mexico, 1845-1847," *The Army Medical Bulletin*, undated, 70.

[99] *The Picayune*, New Orleans, Louisiana, Feb. 21, 1848, 18.

[100] Ibid, May 22, 1848, 169.

The place where all these deceased soldiers were buried seems to have gone unrecorded but a letter written by Lt. Theodore Talbot of the 1st Artillery Regiment on March 19, 1848 mentions one possibility:

Last Thursday afternoon, four Companies of our Regt. had to perform the melancholy part of funeral escort to the remains of Lt. Co. [George W.] Allen of the 2nd Infy, who died the day previous of Pneumonia and fever. I had the command of Capt. [John H.] Winder's Company: the whole escort, commanded by Maj. [Joseph H.] Lamotte. He was buried at the "Camp Santo," ½ a mile from the City. The funeral Service was read by an officer of his regiment. Firing three vollies over his grave, we filed from the grave yard gates, when our band struck up a lively air and we marched in quick time, back again to the City. But the gayest air and step will not serve to banish from our minds the thought that we too are mortal and that many who returned keeping pace with that gay music would yet be borne back accompanied by its most solemn dirges. There is a Chapel in the middle of the "Camp Santo," but being on the line of the American investment it is much injured by the missiles of the Mexicans.[101]

Puente de Nacional (National Bridge), Vera Cruz

On August 12, 1847, as they were coming up from Vera Cruz to join Scott's advance on Mexico City, troops under the command of Major F. T. Lally were ambushed by Mexican forces at the *Puente de Nacional* or National Bridge, which still spans the Rio del Plan to this very day. In the ensuing skirmish, which was later called simply the "Affair at the National Bridge," four Americans were killed, including the son of Gen. David E. Twiggs. Seven other soldiers were mortally wounded. Where these men were buried is unknown but it is not unlikely that their remains were interred near the spot where they fell. It is equally probable, owing to the status of his father, that the body of George Twiggs, who was "acting in the staff of the commanding

---

[101] Robert V. Hine and Savoie Lottinville, *Soldier in the West: Letters of Theodore Talbot During His Service in California, Mexico, and Oregon, 1845-53* (Norman, Oklahoma: University of Oklahoma Press, 1972), 66-67.

officer" at the time of his death and "was expecting a commission and to be aid-de-camp to General Twiggs"[102] was later disinterred and returned to the U.S.

In September and October 1847 a regiment of Maryland and District of Columbia Volunteers, were camped temporarily at the National Bridge. During the short time they guarded the site, the regiment lost no fewer than eight men, who are also probably buried in the vicinity[103].

During the latter part of the war, the National Bridge was guarded by a garrison of Tennesseans. One observer, who visited the encampment, called it "very sickly," and recalled seeing "numerous low mounds, in each of which reposed half a score of silent tenants." These, he remarked, "whispered to us a mournful story."[104] Whether these were the graves of deceased volunteers or Lally's men who perished in the affair of August 1847 (or both) is uncertain. Around this same time, a nearby house, apparently, was used as a hospital.[105]

Cerro Gordo & Plan del Rio, Vera Cruz

The Battle of Cerro Gordo, which occurred on April 18, 1847, took eighty-seven American lives.[106] Even before the engagement had concluded, General Winfield Scott ordered a field hospital to be established in the nearby village of Plan del Rio. Here the wounded were treated while burial details tended to the dead.[107] One man who was present described the scene:

The hospitals at Plan presented a pitiful spectacle; all the little cane

---

[102] *Senate Executive Document No. 8*, 491-492.

[103] Wells, 34, 44, 50, 54, & 61.

[104] M'Sherry, 194.

[105] Original letter to Lieut. G. W. Clutter from H. H. Higgins, dated April 1, 1851, in the possession of Ms. Barbara Millner, Reston, Virginia. Ms. Millner supplied the author with a copy of this letter, which describes a picture of the National Bridge drawn by Higgins that is now in possession of Duke University.

[106] *Niles'*, January 15, 1848, 312.

[107] Duncan, p. 82; Raphael Semmes, *Service Afloat and Ashore During the Mexican War* (Cincinnat: W. H. Moore & Co., 1851), 174.

buildings on the side of the road were filled with wounded men, who were ranged along on blankets, stretched on the bare earth. They lay in their ordinary clothing, in many instances stiff with blood. In every possible way they were wounded. Walking around were some who had been slightly wounded. Some were delirious and groaning with pain, some dying, some dead. The burial ground nearby was continually receiving victims.[108]

When the remainder of the army went forward to Jalapa, the most severely wounded were left at Plan del Rio in the care of Assistant Surgeon Henry H. Steiner. One company of the 1st Regiment of Artillery, under the command of Capt. John B. Magruder, were detailed to remain behind also, to help care for the wounded and to bury the dead.[109]

Two weeks after the battle, Naval Lieut. Raphael Semmes stopped to rest in Plan del Rio, on his way from Vera Cruz to join Scott's army in Jalapa. Here, in the shadow of the mountains where so many of his fellow Americans had been killed, he saw numerous signs of the recent struggle: Mexican cannons lying spiked in the road, their wooden carriages destroyed, the blackened remains of huts burned to the ground, and the "newly-made graves on the left of the road [that] showed where such of the wounded as had died after being borne from the field of battle, had been buried." "The poor fellows who tenanted them," he mused, "had already been forgotten; there being no mark by which one grave could be distinguished from another."[110]

Jalapa, Vera Cruz

On April 21, 1847, following the army's bloodless conquest of Jalapa, Assistant Surgeon Adam N. McClaren established a hospital in some old convent buildings. Apparently, soldiers who died there were buried in an existing Mexican grave yard. In his postwar memoirs, Private George Ballentine of the 1st Artillery Regiment

---

[108] Duncan, 82.

[109] Ibid.

[110] Semmes, p. 174.

recalled the day he was called upon to perform burial duty at Jalapa:

> About a week after our arrival, I was sent, with a party of men, to dig graves for six of our own deceased comrades, who had died in consequence of wounds received in the late action at Cerro Gordo. In digging these graves we remarked, though we dug up a number of skulls and bones of the human skeleton, that there was not a fragment of a coffin visible. From this circumstance we inferred that the poorer classes, in this part of Mexico, dispense with coffins in burying their dead.[111]

The soldiers were confirmed in their conclusion, recalled Ballentine, when, upon leaving the grave-yard they passed a Mexican funeral procession and saw that the deceased, a young child, was being borne to its grave resting only on a board.[112]

Shortly after Lieutenant Semmes arrived in Jalapa he witnessed two funerals. One, held in the city's cathedral and attended by Generals Scott and Twiggs, and Colonels Childs and Hitchcock, was for a Mexican officer, "a captain in the 4th Light-infantry, who had been mortally wounded at the battle of Cerro Gordo." On the very same day, Semmes recalled, a funeral was held for a "lieutenant of Illinois volunteers, who died also of his wounds." The young naval officer also remembered the death of Capt. Stevens T. Mason of the Mounted Rifle Regiment, who had been tended by a pretty young *señorita* until his death on May 15, 1847.[113]

According to Semmes, U.S. soldiers who died during the occupation of Jalapa were buried "on the heights north of the town, in, as one might fancy, the Elysian Fields of the ancients." From the balcony of his quarters, he wrote, he "could see the [funeral] processions, and hear the roll of the muffled drum, and the long and

---

[111] George Ballentine, *Autobiography of an English Soldier in the United States Army* (New York: Stringer & Townsend, 1854), 206.

[112] Ibid.

[113] Semmes, p. 204. Semmes may have been mistaken in regard to the regiment to which the American officer was attached. The only Illinois officer mortally wounded at Cerro Gordo was Lieut. Richard Murphy, who died on April 20, two weeks before Semmes arrived in Jalapa.

mournful cadences of the shrill fife, as the comrades of the deceased, with arms reversed and funeral step, followed their late brother to his honorable resting place, beneath the acacia and the rose."[114]

Perote, Vera Cruz

As Scott's army marched toward the interior of Mexico, the city of Perote was taken without firing a shot by forces under the command of Gen. William J. Worth on April 22, 1847. Afterward, the infamous old *Castillo de Perote*, formerly a prison (a use to which it has since been returned), was made into a hospital for the sick and wounded. Apparently, it was a dreadful place. In his memoirs, Private Ballentine estimated that for several months following its conversion from a place of incarceration to a shelter for the sick and wounded, men died there at the rate of twelve per day. There were so many, he noted, that the usual military funeral formalities ceased to be observed. "Wrapped in the blankets in which they died," he wrote, "they were carted out and thrown into pits dug for the purpose daily outside of the garrison."[115]

Ballentine's recollection of Perote is corroborated by Pvt. Richard Coulter of the Pennsylvania Volunteers who wrote in his private journal that the soldiers who daily died in the overcrowded castle numbered "from eight to ten a day, often being as high as fifteen in a single day." The Pennsylvanian estimated that during the year that Perote was occupied by U.S. forces, over 2,000 men were buried around the ditch or moat that surrounded the forbidding stone fortress. Burying the dead in their blankets, he noted, was necessitated by there being no wood available with which to build coffins.[116]

Marine Surgeon Richard M'Sherry was another witness to Perote's unhealthy clime. "Outside of the walls [of Castle Perote]," he

---

[114] Ibid, 204-205.

[115] Ballentine, 233.

[116] Allen Peskin, Volunteers: *The Mexican War Journals of Private Richard Coulter and Sergeant Thomas Barclay, Company E, Second Pennsylvania Infantry* (Kent, Ohio: Kent State University Press, 1991), 115 & 307.

later recalled, "immediately in rear of our camp, is a double line of mounds, where repose all the perishable parts of hundreds of our brave citizen soldiers." "They have fallen by the scores," he added, "not upon the battlefield, but from the ravages of disease."[117]

Lt. Col. William Preston of the 4th Regiment of Kentucky Volunteers who passed through the city twice, once in the fall of 1847 and again in the spring of 1848, likewise attested to the deadliness of the hospital at Perote. The first time he saw the place, his regiment had just come up from Vera Cruz on their way to Puebla. They later formed part of the garrison at Mexico City. While at Perote, the Kentuckian later wrote in his memoirs, he recalled seeing a "long line of American graves on the east flank of the castle." These, he remarked, attested to "the dreadful mortality that prevailed there among our troops." During his second visit to Perote, in April 1848, Preston chanced to meet Lt. Col. Isaac G. Seymour of the Battalion of Georgia Volunteers, who "informed me that about twenty-six hundred American soldiers had died there since he held it." "As evidence of its unhealthiness," Preston further remarked, Lieutenant Colonel Seymour "stated that his battalion had been mustered into service on the 28th of October, 1847, four hundred nineteen strong; that in six months he had lost two hundred men by death; that at the time he had but forty-two men for duty, the rest being in the hospital, or languishing from disease."[118]

Puebla, Puebla

After Puebla was occupied by Scott's forces on May 15, 1847, Surgeon William J. Barry set up a hospital in a combination of convent and other public buildings which soon became overcrowded with soldiers suffering and dying, principally from diarrhea,[119] even though, according to one soldier, it was "kept in perfect order" with

---

[117] M'Sherry, 50.
[118] William Preston, *Journal in Mexico* (Paris, France: Privately printed, 1920), 22.
[119] Duncan, 90.

"everything clean" and lacking "the disagreeable smell incident to all hospitals." [120] Clean or not, soldiers died there in large numbers. "One could not walk far through the streets of Puebla without hearing the mournful strains of the soldier's funeral procession," recalled Pvt. George Ballentine.[121] Other soldiers confirmed this sad scenario. "Not a day passes but I see from one to four or even five funerals pass my quarters," wrote Lt. Ralph W. Kirkham, "daily some poor fellow goes to his long home."[122] Neither of these men, however, or any others apparently, recorded the location of any American burial sites in Puebla.

In his journal, a volunteer described an incident that occurred at Puebla in 1848 that revealed another reason for the trepidation some men felt about leaving the remains of their comrades interred in a country that was not only foreign to them, but hostile as well:

> Lieut. [John] Sturgeon of Fayette County…died at Puebla while we were there. His body embalmed was laid in the vaults of the church. It was intended to take the remains home but the villanous Mexicans stole away the coffin. The object of those people in thus violating the hallowed precincts of the tomb is in consistency with other features of their character. It is the low despicable feeling of gain which induces them hyena like to dig up the grave and break open the coffin of the dead. And the blanket and clothing of the corpse is their reward.[123]

When Scott's army began its advance on Mexico City in August 1847, the two regiments of Pennsylvanians were left behind to garrison the town. During the siege of Puebla, which occurred in October, following the fall of Mexico City, they lost seven men to enemy fire. Losses to illness were much higher. Before the Pennsylvania men departed for Mexico City toward the end of 1847,

---

[120] Peskin, p. 124.

[121] Ballentine, p. 233.

[122] Robert Ryal Miller, ed., *The Mexican War Journal & Letters of Ralph W. Kirkham* (College Station, Texas: Texas A.&M. University Press, 1991), 22.

[123] Peskin, 251.

nearly one-hundred sons of the Keystone State had been laid to rest at Puebla.[124] Other volunteer regiments, stationed in the city for varying lengths of time, seem to have fared no better. Although the precise number of Americans who are buried there is unknown, it must surely be in the hundreds.

The Valley of Mexico

Some of the deadliest military engagements of the U.S.-Mexican War were fought during August and September 1847 in the Valley of Mexico. The first of these, the battles of Contreras and Churubusco, which took place on August 19 and 20, together resulted in 164 U.S. fatalities. At the conclusion of the Battle of El Molino del Rey, which occurred on September 8, 1847, 201 Americans were dead or dying. A week later, following the final fighting that led to the fall of the capital and its occupation by U.S. forces, another 178 Americans had been killed or mortally wounded. The total: 543.[125]

Accounts are sketchy concerning the locations of the graves of American soldiers who were killed at Contreras and Churubusco. A Pennsylvania volunteer, visiting Contreras after the battle, told of seeing "a large mound of earth surmounted by a cross under which reposes the Mexican dead"[126] but failed to mention any corresponding U.S. burial site. He also witnessed a somewhat morbid scene at San Angel, the village where his regiment was quartered. "The surgeons of our brigade," he wrote on March 12, 1848, "disinterred the bodies of the deserters buried in the field opposite our quarters for the purpose of getting the skeletons."[127] Presumably, the remains of these particular men, members of the infamous *San Patricio* Battalion, were to be used for medical research.

Lt. Ralph W. Kirkham of the 6th Infantry Regiment was present on September 9, 1847, when the bodies of U.S. soldiers killed at

---

[124] State of Pennsylvania, *Pennsylvania Archives*, 6th Series, vol. 10, 249-458.
[125] *Niles'*, January 15, 1848, 312.
[126] Peskin, 253.
[127] Ibid., 273.

Molino del Rey the day before were buried at nearby Tacubuya. In his journal, the young West Point graduate recorded his impressions of their funeral:

> We buried today the officers and soldiers who fell in the murderous affair of yesterday. One hundred and seventeen poor but gallant fellows lie side by side in a field on the side hill in rear of the bishop's palace and in sight of the battlefield. Mr. McCarty performed the service over them, and not an eye was dry, for we had all of us lost those whom we loved. They were buried with military honors, and I trust their memories will remain fresh in the hearts of those of us who knew them and witnessed their gallantry upon this as well as other occasions.[128]

An American newspaper also reported the burial of "the honored dead" of Molino del Rey, who "were interred with the rites of war on the heights of Tacubuya." An Episcopal service was read, noted the paper, and General Worth attended.[129]

On September 11, while his regiment was still positioned at Tacubuya, Lieutenant Kirkham recorded the death and burial of two American officers who were mortally wounded at Molino del Rey:

> Lieutenant [John G.] Burbank died yesterday, and we followed him to the grave today. He was shot in the left side, and I thought the wound was not dangerous, for I saw him on the battlefield and he was cheerful and said he suffered very little pain…Today Captain E. K. Smith has also died from his wound; he was shot through the head and there was little hope he would recover.[130]

Following the fall of Mexico City on September 14, 1847, General Winfield Scott's victorious little army began to settle in for an indefinite stay—one that ended up lasting several months. Almost immediately, army hospitals were established at several points throughout the Mexican capital. These places included the Bishop's

---

[128] Miller, 59.

[129] Duncan, 104.

[130] Ibid., 61.

Palace near the Molino del Rey, the Governor's Palace, the College of Mines, the Iturbide Palace, the Palace of the Inquisition, and the Convent of Saint Isabella. There were also army hospitals at San Augustine, Mixcoac, Tacubuya, San Angel—small villages located to the south or west of the city.[131]

In addition to battle deaths, during the ten months the capital and its environs were occupied, between 200 and 600 U.S. soldiers died in the Valley of Mexico. Most were victims of illness. Some were murdered.[132] On September 21, 1847, Lieutenant Kirkham wrote: "Hardly a day passes without one or more of our soldiers being assassinated. They get intoxicated and wander into bye streets and almost invariably are stabbed."[133]

On September 23, 1847, Lieutenant Kirkham revealed the location of the burial place of at least one American officer when he wrote of attending the funeral of Lt. Rudolph F. Ernst, who had been wounded at Molino del Rey. Although it was hoped that Ernst would recover, noted Kirkham, "he died last night and was buried in the [cemetery of the] convent of San Fernando, [established by] an order of friars, with the usual Roman Catholic ceremonies."[134]

Protestant soldiers such as Lieutenant Kirkham (an Episcopalian) often viewed the Roman Catholic faith with a jaundiced eye. When Lt. Gustavus Gardner of the Massachusetts Regiment of Volunteers. died in March 1848, Pvt. Richard Coulter, a non-Catholic, attended his funeral. In his journal, Coulter described what was to him an altogether strange and repugnant ceremony:

[Gardner] was buried in a Mexican graveyard near a little old chapel

---

[131] Duncan, 100, 104 & 108.

[132] The lower figure is based on the official figure of 750 Americans buried in the Mexico City National Cemetery. Subtracting the 543 battle fatalities who were supposed to have been interred there, leaves 207 that died of other causes. However, rosters of the volunteer regiments that occupied the capital reveal that as many as 600 men may have died in Mexico City and its environs. A count of deaths among the regulars would undoubtedly increase that figure.

[133] Miller, 68.

[134] Ibid.

about a half mile from this village [San Angel] where several others of his regiment, Catholics, were buried, and by paying for the ground, respect is insured for the grave. He, being a Catholic, the old priest of the chapel officiated at the funeral. The old priest was a native Mexican, almost pure Indian blood. A little ragged urchin preceded him in chanting. The chapel bells tolled during the entire ceremony. Considerable mummery was gone through, a quantity of holy water used upon his coffin and the assembly, when it was placed in the grave with military honors. It was an odd scene and decidedly ludicrous. His chanting was most terrible.[135]

It appears that Protestant officers who died during the occupation of the capital were most frequently buried in the English Cemetery, which had been established some years earlier for the interment of British citizens who died in Mexico. This burial ground was located on what was then the outskirts of the city, at the junction of the westernmost end of the San Cosmé Causeway (now the Parque Via James Sullivan) and the northern end of the aqueduct (now the Calle Melchor Ocampo/Circuito Interior) that led south to Chapultepec. In his journal, Lieutenant Kirkham recorded the deaths of four officers who were buried in the English Cemetery: Col. James S. McIntosh of the 5th Infantry Regiment, who died on September 28, 1847 from wounds received at Molino del Rey; Lt. John D. Bacon of the 6th Infantry Regiment and Lt. Muscoe L. Shackleford of the 2d Artillery Regiment, both of whom were wounded in battle and died on October 12; and Assistant Surgeon William Roberts of the Georgia Battalion of Volunteers, who died October 13 from wounds he received at Molino del Rey.[136] An article reporting the funerals of the latter three was published in the *Daily American Star*, in its issue of October 15, 1847.[137]

The *Star*, an occupation newspaper printed in both Spanish and English, reported that Col. Trueman B. Ransom of the 9th Infantry Regiment, who was killed at the Battle of Chapultepec on September

---

[135] Peskin, 275-276.

[136] Miller, p. 72; Heitman, 179, 836 & 876.

[137] *Daily American Star*, October 15, 1847, 2.

13, 1847, was another American officer who had been buried in the English cemetery[138] and a later edition of the paper revealed that the body of Lt. Perrin Watson of the 14th Infantry Regiment, who died January 3, 1848, was interred at the Convent of Santo Domingo.[139]

Córdoba and Orizaba, Vera Cruz

During the latter part of 1847 and early 1848, the towns of Córdoba and Orizaba, located near the volcanic peak of Orizaba, were occupied by troops from Alabama and Michigan. The single known account of their stay there, written by one of the Alabama men, does not mention the deaths or burials of any soldiers although the battalion to which he belonged lost 14 men at Orizaba, most to chronic diarrhea. None of the Alabamians died at Códorba. The Michigan men's losses are not known.

---

[138] Ibid., October 31, 1847, 2.
[139] Ibid., January 4, 1848, 3.

Chapter 3
Disinterment & Reburials
in the U.S.

Notwithstanding that Thomas Bangs Thorpe surely believed it at the time he wrote about Colonel Cross' funeral, the burial ground beside Fort Texas (later re-named Fort Brown) was not to be the Colonel's final resting place. Although there were no laws or regulations in 1846 requiring the return deceased soldiers' remains to their families, there was nothing to prevent private citizens from retrieving the body themselves or paying for it to be done. Although it is uncertain who arranged it, Colonel Cross was but the first of several U.S. officers that died during the War with Mexico, whose bones were disinterred from their original graves and reburied elsewhere.

In November 1846, *Niles' National Register* reported that "the remains of Col. Cross, the first victim of the Mexican war, a gallant Marylander by birth, and...officer who had no superior in the department in which he served, reached Baltimore from the banks of the Rio Grande, last week." "The relics," the paper noted, were escorted by an honor guard to Baltimore's railroad depot, where they were loaded on a train bound for Washington, D.C.. Upon arrival in the nation's capital, they were taken to the Congressional Cemetery, where Cross' "imposing" second funeral was attended by a large crowd of people that included President James K. Polk, "the heads of departments, public officers, officers of the army and navy, the civil authorities, and members of the community, amongst whom he had so long lived."[140]

In late November 1846, Private Scribner and five of his comrades returned to Point Isabel where they spent the night. The next morning, recalled the young soldier:

> ...we witnessed the thrilling spectacle of the disinterment of the remains of Major Ringgold, for the Baltimore committee. The coffin was escorted to the quartermaster's depot, by a company of regulars. Others formed a procession in the rear, and all marched to the tune of "Adestes Fiedeles," accompanied by the roaring of one eighteen pounder. Having arrived at the destined place, the body was removed to a leaden coffin. It was so decayed we could form no idea of its form or features.[141]

Following short stops in New Orleans and Mobile, Alabama, the committee assigned to bring home Ringgold's body reached Baltimore in late December. His second funeral, held on Tuesday, December 22, 1846, was described in great detail by *Niles' National Register*. It was a grand affair. "The streets [of Baltimore]," reported the paper, "were thronged so as to be almost impassable from one end of the city to the other" and "the windows of most of the houses were taken out to accommodate the spectators." After lying in state in the rotunda of the Exchange Building, the war hero's coffin was carried through the city's streets, accompanied by a military honor guard. "The music of a dozen or more bands," along with "the mournful appendages of flags displayed at half mast in innumerable directions, the toiling bells, the muffled drums, the dead march, the gloom that everywhere pervaded the dense throng of living beings," the paper remarked, "spoke a language to the heart that needed no interpreter."[142]

Singled out for special attention was Sergeant Kelly, a member of Ringgold's company of "flying artillery" who had "left his good right arm" on "the field of Palo Alto." Kelly, it seems, was particularly

---

[140] *Niles' National Register*, Baltimore, Maryland, November 28, 1846, 208.
[141] Ibid, 38.
[142] *Niles' National Register*, Baltimore, Maryland, January 2, 1847, 273.

devoted to his commanding officer. When the Baltimore committee arrived at Point Isabel to disinter Ringgold's body, the sergeant had "applied for permission to accompany the remains of his deceased friend and beloved commander to their last resting place," although the stump of his arm had not yet completely healed. During the slow procession to Greenmount Cemetery, he led a representative rider-less horse ("The remains of the real steed," remarked the paper, "lay mouldering on the battle field.") and no one, reported *Niles'*, "was more deeply affected on the occasion, or was an object of more general interest and sympathy"[143]

Remarkably, Capt. John Page, who suffered an especially gruesome wound, outlived Ringgold by several weeks. On May 16th, after hearing a premature report that Page had died, Lieutenant Dana wrote in a letter to his wife: "Poor fellow, it perhaps is for the best. He could never have spoke or have known a pleasant moment again. The whole lower part of his face - lower jaw, mouth, teeth, tongue, and all—were carried away by a cannonball."[144] After lingering for more than two months, Page was on his way home when he passed away in his wife's arms aboard the steamboat *Missouri* at 3 o'clock in the morning on July 12, 1846. The following day, at Jefferson Barracks, Missouri, he was laid to rest during a funeral service that was attended by a newly-enlisted regiment of Illinois volunteers who were about to embark for the seat of the war. Among the soldiers who witnessed the ceremonies for Page was Pvt. Thomas D. Tennery. In the journal he had recently begun to keep, Tennery wrote:

The funeral was a grand but solemn scene. The regiment paraded and marched out in platoons, until the head of the column reached the road, then wheeled to the left and halted at the church. We, being not well, went on and stepped into the church, where the corpse lay, before the chaplain who was making some appropriate remarks for the congregation, and commending his wife and children to the

---

[143] Ibid.
[144] Ferrell, 75.

friend of the widow, and father of the orphans. After prayer the coffin was carried and placed in the hearse. At this moment the sun was sinking behind the western horizon encircled by golden edged clouds, the wind blew gently from the north waving the colors toward the graveyard. The band of music accompanied the hearse to the grave playing a funeral air, followed by the regiment. When the music ceased, all halted, the pall-bearers approached the hearse, bore the body to its long home, three volleys blazed over the open grave, breaking the death like silence, and illuminating the approaching dusk. A few of us filled the grave and left him to sleep until____no more and the trumpet shall again call forth.[145]

In June 1995, while passing through Missouri, this writer stopped at Jefferson Barracks for the purpose of locating Page's grave. Anyone expecting to find it marked by a monument of substantial size, as befitting one of the first fatalities of the U.S.-Mexican War, will be disappointed. A small white marble slab, indistinguishable from the thousands of others that stand nearby in neat rows like silent sentinels, is all there is.[146]

The bodies of at least some of the officers who died and were buried at Monterey were eventually returned to the U.S. for re-interment. Among these were Colonel Watson, commanding officer of the Baltimore and District of Columbia Battalion, Capt. Randolph Ridgely, a regular army officer who survived the battle but died after being thrown from his horse, striking his head on a paving stone in the streets of Monterey, Capt. Isaac Holmes of the Georgia Volunteers, Capt. Richard A. Gillespie of the Texas Mounted Volunteers, and Lt. Richard H. Graham of the 4th Infantry. The bodies of two Maryland-born Texas Volunteers, Pvt. Herman Thomas, who had been mortally wounded on September 22, 1846, and a man named Pearson, were also disinterred from their battlefield graves.

Capt. Franklin Smith of the Mississippi Volunteers was still at Camargo on Monday, December 28, 1846, when "Lieut. Mills of

---

[145] Livingston-Little, 7-8.
[146] Personal observation by the author, June 1995.

Baltimore arrived from Monterey bringing with him the mortal remains of Col. Watson, Capt. Randolph Ridgely, Thomas, Pierson [sic], Graham, Capt. Gillespie and some one else I forget who—there are seven corpses." (The man whose name Smith could not remember was Captain Holmes.) The following day, while the coffins were stacked near the Rio San Juan, waiting to be loaded on a steamboat bound for the mouth of the Rio Grande, Smith wandered down from his office to take a look. Afterward, in his journal, he wrote reflectively:

> Went down this morning to one of our tarpaulins where the bodies of the illustrious dead are deposited awaiting the arrival and departure of some of the steamers (there happens to be none here now). There lie the poor fellows whose names just now are more in the hearts and thoughts of men than any other names known to history— there they lie in rough square boxes of coarse pine plank— heaped up among other boxes of quarter master's stores awaiting transportation! Muskets, old escopetas, swords, and broken lances (which some of those who survived the battle are carrying home for relicks [sic]) are scattered loosely upon and around the boxes—a single sentinel of the quarter guard is stationed at the entrance of the tarpaulin frame! I walked in and surveyed these boxes and accompaniments! It was impossible to feel scarcely a single heroic emotion so much does the sight affect the imagination. Hearing the corpses had arrived I went to see them foolishly expecting I dont [sic] know how or why to find elegant coffins! When I saw the rough pine boxes laying about as the convenience of the hands required— (like the ordinary gun boxes of the ordnance department) among barrels corn sacks and undistinguished that precious and heroic dust from the trash around I felt how vain and futile the attempt to impart the honors of the living to the dead![147]

Continuing to write in his journal, Smith expressed an opinion that seems to have been less commonly held, one that no doubt resulted from the shock of seeing the seven coffins stacked under the tarpaulin as if they were nothing more than cargo: Instead of sending the bodies home, he now thought, perhaps they ought to remain

---

[147] Chance, *The Mexican War Journal of Captain Franklin Smith*, 149-150.

where they were originally buried. "To prolong our interest in dull inanimate matter," he mused, "after 'the heavenly flame' which gave it life and lustre—this soul—has fled! Better poor fellows that they had been left in the gory bed where they fell under the blue vault of the cloudless skies [and] above them was the sublime mountains[,] the witnesses of their heroism around them." Smith recalled the time when he visited the Monterey battlefield and "stood on the height above the Bishop's Palace where Gillespie fell" contemplating "the humble grave of rude stone which his fellow soldiers had carved out of the mountain rock and the spot where it was crimsoned by his life's blood." It was there, wrote the Mississippian, that Gillespie "fought, there he bled, there he died and there he ought to have rested forever!"[148]

As his emotions swept over him, Smith went on to imagine a future when "many an American" would have ascended "that sacred height and holding in his hand the eulogy of Governor Henderson [of Texas] muse long on the virtues of Gillespie while he stood beside the tomb." "Now," he lamented, "half of the charm[,] half of the interest of the spot is broken and dissipated forever!" Questioning the decision to disinter the remains of the celebrated Texan, Smith concluded vehemently: "I know not by whose direction Gillespie was removed—but if by the order of anyone but his family—however noble and generous the feeling which prompted it - it was in my humble opinion a mistaken act of friendship and in exceedingly bad taste."[149]

Smith's feelings notwithstanding, the seven coffins were eventually taken to the mouth of the Rio Grande by steamboat and from there to New Orleans. On the evening of January 7, 1847, the steamer *Alabama* arrived at the "Crescent City." There, the remains of eight dead soldiers were off-loaded, Lt. Eugene Boyle of the Maryland and D.C. Volunteers having died at sea on January 2nd during the passage from Texas. By torch light, their coffins were

---

[148] Ibid.
[149] Ibid.

carried to the city arsenal, to await further transportation. While they were being carried through the city streets, reported *Niles' National Register*, "the flags in all the public places" were flown "at half mast and the mournful minute guns from the place d'Armes and from Lafayette square" announced "the progress of the procession."[150]

The next morning, following ceremonies commemorating the anniversary of the Battle of New Orleans, the coffins of all but Holmes and Gillespie, whose bodies were sent to Georgia and Texas respectively, were once again accompanied through the streets of New Orleans by "a military and civic procession" which "made an impressive appearance." At wharf-side, they were placed aboard the brig *C. H. Rogers*, bound for Baltimore.[151]

The *Rogers* arrived in Baltimore harbor late on Sunday, January 30, 1847. As at New Orleans, the coffins were met by an honor guard, which escorted them to "their several places of resting, until the day fixed for their removal to the cemetery, Monday, the 8th of February." Watson's remains, reported *Niles'*, were taken "to his late residence," while those of Ridgely "were escorted to the armory of the artillerists."[152]

The remains of Herman Thomas, noted the newspaper, "were escorted to the residence of his grandmother, in Fayette street." They were afterward taken by a committee of citizens to Harford County, where, on February 9th, they were "interred with military honors and every demonstration of respect, in the grave yard of Spesutia church." The paper made no mention of what was done with the body of Pearson.[153]

The coffins containing the remains of lieutenants Graham and Boyle did not stay in Baltimore long. Upon arrival, they "were delivered in charge to the committee from Washington" who "conveyed [them]...to that city, and there they were interred with

---

[150] *Niles' National Register*, Baltimore, Maryland, February 13, 1847, 371.
[151] Ibid.
[152] Ibid.
[153] Ibid.

military honors."[154]

The joint funeral of Watson and Ridgely, held on February 8, 1847, was favored by good weather. It began at "an early hour," reported *Niles'*, when "minute guns commenced firing, the bells of the city were tolled, and flags on various public buildings and the shipping were suspended at half-mast." Baltimore's streets were lined with "thousands...who were put out to honor the illustrious and gallant dead" as a procession, which included Governor Pratt and other Maryland state officials, the Mayor of Baltimore, members of Congress, and numerous civic and military organizations, made its way from the capitol to Greenmount Cemetery. "The hearses with the remains of the dead," noted the newspaper, Ridgely first, then Watson, "were drawn...by six white horses, richly caparisoned." Over each coffin was folded an American flag. Albert Hart, a private of the Maryland and D.C. Volunteers who had lost his arm in the Battle of Monterey, walked close behind Watson's hearse "bearing the standard of his country." Capt. Samuel Walker of the Texas Volunteers, a Maryland native who was already noteworthy for his feats of daring during the opening campaigns of the war, also took part in the procession.[155]

At Greenmount Cemetery, where the body of Maj. Samuel Ringgold had been interred only a few months earlier, the coffin containing the remains of Ridgely was "deposited without any ceremonies being observed" in a temporary vault. "The funeral cortege then proceeded to the vault where the remains of Col. Watson were deposited." reported *Niles'*, where a "deeply solemn" ceremony was conducted, causing "many a silent tear [to be] dropped in memory of the lamented dead."[156]

Not surprisingly, the bodies of several prominent officers killed at Buena Vista were later disinterred and taken back to the United States for reburial. When the Arkansas Mounted Volunteers left

---

[154] Ibid.
[155] Ibid.
[156] Ibid.

Saltillo in June 1847, near the end of their term of enlistment, a special detail was sent to the grave-yard to locate and remove Colonel Yell's tin coffin, which was taken by his soldiers to the mouth of the Rio Grande. The remains of Captain Porter and Private Pelham were also retrieved from their graves. From Texas, the bodies of the three men accompanied the Arkansas regiment to New Orleans, then on to Little Rock. On August 3, 1847, Colonel Yell was buried in the cemetery at Fayetteville, his home town. The body of Captain Porter was buried at Batesville, Arkansas. Private Pelham, whose grave is marked with a plain stone, was laid to rest in Mount Holly Cemetery in Little Rock.[157]

John Pelham was one of the few but not the only enlisted man killed at the Battle of Buena Vista whose remains were reburied in the United States. When the 2nd Indiana Regiment was preparing to leave Mexico toward the end of May 1847, wrote Private Scribner, "we received a request from the citizens of New Albany to bring home the four bodies of our fallen comrades." The individuals to whom the request referred were, presumably, Francis Bailey, Charles H. Goff, Warren Robinson, and Apollos J. Stevens. Scribner confessed that the men of his company had already considered retrieving the bodies, but had "given it up as impossible." "But now it must be done he," he recorded in his journal on May 15th, "and preparations are being made for their transportation." Remarking that "the Mexicans are inferior mechanics, and material is scarce," Scribner added that "we shall have to use tin instead of lead for coffins, as the latter is not to be had."[158]

---

[157] Allen, p. 15 & 42; Robert L. Duncan, *Reluctant General: The Life and Times of Albert Pike* (New York: E. P. Dutton and Co., 1961), 129. In June 1872, Yell's remains were disinterred and buried for a third and final time, in the Masonic Cemetery at Fayetteville.

[158] Scribner, 72-73; Indiana Adjutant General's Office, *Indiana in the Mexican War* (Indianapolis: Wm. B. Burford, 1908), 371. A fifth member of Scribner's company, Pvt. Larkin Cunningham, died on March 6, 1847. He is not listed as one of the wounded. In all likelihood, Cunningham succumbed to an illness. Because Scribner does not mention him in his journal, it seems safe to assume that he was not among the four bodies that the Indiana men carried back to

The Indiana regiment left Buena Vista, where they had been camped since the battle, on May 24, 1847. They arrived at New Albany, Indiana on July 3rd. "On the fifth," wrote Scribner, " we transported to the solemn grave, the remains of our fellow soldiers." They were followed by a procession of the town's citizens who witnessed "the mournful ceremony." Scribner afterward predicted that a "noble monument will mark the resting-place of those who fell in battle."[159]

During the late spring or early summer of 1847, the remains of George Lincoln were also disinterred from the cemetery in Saltillo. Shipped to Boston, they were received by his father Levi Lincoln, a former governor of Massachusetts.[160] Held on July 22nd, the young officer's funeral services, reported the *New Haven Register*, "called out a large concourse of people and the procession was unusually large." At Boston, Mayor Quincy delivered a speech over Lincoln's coffin, which was made of "rich, black walnut" and topped by two swords and "his cap, plume, and belt." Afterward, it was escorted to the train depot by a military guard consisting of six army officers "of the same rank with the deceased." Attached to the casket, which rested atop a funeral carriage draped in black and drawn by four white horses," was "a plain, but rich silver plate" that bore the following inscription: "GEORGE LINCOLN, Capt. 8th reg't inft'y U.S.A., FELL at Buena Vista, Mexico, Feb. 23, 1847. Aged 29 years." Following behind was the very same white horse, decked out in funereal black, "from which he fell at Buena Vista," wearing Lincoln's saddle and holster. His "long military boots, spurred as if for battle," were hung over the horse's back.[161]

Lincoln's horse, "a large muscular animal...nearly white, or very light grey," had been auctioned off after his death. The buyer, who

New Albany.
[159] Scribner, 74-75.
[160] Chance, Jefferson Davis's *Mexican War Regiment*, 111.
[161] *Niles' National Register*, Baltimore, Maryland, August 7, 1847, 365; G. N. Allen, *Incidents & Sufferings in the Mexican War...*(Boston & New York: 1848), 14.

paid $250, was none other than Sarah Borginnes, the famed "Great Western" or "Heroine of Fort Brown." When she learned the name of its original owner she declared her intention to give it to Lincoln's mother as a gift. Upon the departure of the Kentucky Regiment from Saltillo, she "relinquished the horse [to them], by whom it was he was presented to the family of the deceased and forwarded to Boston."[162]

Following the funeral train's arrival at Worcester, Lincoln's home town, his coffin was borne through the streets by a military escort made up of several militia units. Behind the hearse, once again, was his horse, followed by the family of the deceased young man and a concourse of the town's citizens, along with those who had traveled by train from Boston. After funeral services at the First Unitarian Church, the remains of Captain Lincoln were finally laid to rest in Salisbury Cemetery, at a spot, declared one observer, of "simple and quiet beauty; a fit resting place for the honored dead, whose fame is their won monument."[163]

When the 2nd Kentucky Regiment prepared to leave Saltillo, its commanding officer, Maj. Cary H. Fry, directed his men to disinter the bodies of Colonel McKee, Lt. Colonel Clay, Capt. William T. Willis, Lt. Edward M. Vaughn of the Kentucky Mounted Regiment and eleven enlisted men belonging to both regiments who had either perished in the Battle of Buena Vista or died afterward. On their way through Monterey, they also stopped to disinter the remains of Lt. Joseph Powell, who had died there on January 2, 1847. When the Kentuckians arrived at New Orleans, where they were mustered out of federal service, a funeral procession followed the coffins of the dead soldiers, carried on artillery caissons draped in black velvet, through the city's streets. Afterward, the soldiers' remains were loaded aboard the steamboat *Ringgold*, named for another dead hero of the war, which transported them to Louisville. They were afterward taken to Frankfort, where they lay in state in the rotunda of

---

[162] Allen, 13-15.
[163] Ibid, 16.

the state capitol, awaiting reburial in the state cemetery.[164]

On July 27, 1847, at Frankfort, a crowd numbering from 15,000 to 30,000 people gathered to pay tribute to Kentucky's fallen sons with an elaborate funeral service that began at 10 o'clock in the morning with the firing of two cannons. Notwithstanding the short notice of the event and "the intense and almost overpowering heat of the weather [that] prevented many from attending," wrote a reporter for the *Frankfort Commonwealth*, "there came together on that day, the largest concourse of people ever assembled in Kentucky."[165]

The funeral procession, which set out from the capitol building, included Governor William Owlsey and other state officials, fifteen military organizations, members of local clubs and fraternal societies, college students, and citizens in carriages and on foot. A band from Newport Barracks provided the music and a cannon was fired every five minutes as the coffins of the dead soldiers, resting on cannon carriages draped with black cloth, were drawn by horses to the state cemetery, located on a hill overlooking the Kentucky River. Among the dignitaries present at graveside were Senator Henry Clay, who sat with his grandchildren, the orphans of Lt. Colonel Clay, and Richard

---

[164] L. F. Johnson, *The History of Franklin County, Kentucky* (Frankfort: Roberts Printing Co., 1912), 127-128; Steven L. Wright, "Edward H. Hobson," *Green County [Kentucky] Review*, vol. xv, no. 3, Spring 1992, 40; Kentucky Adjutant General, *Report of the Adjutant General of the State of Kentucky: Mexican War Veterans* (Frankfort, Kentucky: Capitol Office, John D. Woods, Public Printer and Binder, 1889), 21-22; *Executive Document No. 8*, 122-126 & 129-131; *Frankfort Cemetery in Kentucky* (Frankfort: The Kentucky Genealogical Society, Inc., 1988), 203-204. Six of the enlisted men made up the entire battle fatality list of Company K, 1st Regiment of Kentucky Mounted Volunteers. They were Cpl. William W. Bayless and privates Henry Carty, Alex. G. Morgan, Nathaniel or Cincinnattus Ramey, William Thwaits, and Clement Jones. Other members of the mounted regiment whose remains were removed to the U.S. were: Pvt. C. B. Thompson of Co. E; Pvt. W. T. or W. C. Green of Co. G, who had been "assassinated at Saltillo, by Mexicans, March 2d [1847]"; and Pvt. Thomas Weigart of Co. I. Another private, Harvey Trotter, had been a member of Co. F, 2nd Regiment of Kentucky Foot Volunteers. It is uncertain to which organization the eleventh enlisted man, Tilford McH. Dozier, was attached.
[165] *Niles' National Register*, Baltimore, Maryland, August 7, 1847, 362; Johnson, 127-128.

Mentor Johnson, who had served as Vice-President of the United States during the Van Buren administration. Lexington lawyer John C. Breckinridge, who would later hold the office of Vice-President under Buchanan and run for President against Lincoln in 1860, was the keynote speaker.[166]

During the same summer that Colonel McKee and his men were laid to rest in the Kentucky State Cemetery, the trustees of the city of Frankfort and Franklin County authorities together appropriated a sum of money to be used to retrieve the remains of certain Franklin County men who had been killed during the Battle of Buena Vista or died afterward. Benjamin C. Milam, who had recently returned to Kentucky after serving as captain of Company C, 1st Regiment of Kentucky Mounted Volunteers, was chosen to carry out the task. On his return journey to Mexico Milam passed through New Orleans, where Ruben C. Hawkins, a former private who had served under Captain Chambers in McKee's regiment, joined him. Together, the two men continued on to Saltillo where Hawkins helped identify the graves of the men he had helped to bury. Milam left Mexico first, leaving Hawkins to finish the job. When he set out for Kentucky in late August or early September, the former enlisted man brought with him the remains of twelve of his dead comrades: privates J. F. Ellingwood, Robert Latta, James Seston, and John Sanders—all of Milam's company; Sgt. Henry Wolf and privates Samuel or L. B. Bartlett, William Blackwell, and Major Updike—all of Chamber's company; and Cpl. Henry Edwards and privates. Enoch G. Burton, Abram Goodpaster, and Yves J. Thoreau—all of Captain Turpin's company.[167]

When Hawkins arrived at Louisville, Milam was at the wharf, along with Captain Chambers and a militia unit, the McKee Guards, to greet him and to take charge of the bodies. From Louisville, they

---

[166] Ibid. ; *An Address on the Occasion of the Burial of the Kentucky Volunteers...(*Lexington, Kentucky: the Observer and Reporter Office, 1847).
[167] Johnson, p. 127; *Frankfort Cemetery in Kentucky, pp. 203-204; Executive Document No. 8,* 122-126 & 129-131.

were transported to Frankfort where on September 16, 1847, on the grounds of the state cemetery, the deceased soldiers were interred with full military honors beside their comrades who had been buried there two months earlier. Although this second funeral was not as well attended as the one in July, the crowd was still sizable. Approximately 3,000 people attended, mostly residents of Franklin county and its outlying communities.[168]

Col. John J. Hardin, who died leading his regiment of Illinois Volunteers at Buena Vista was similarly honored at his home town of Jacksonville, Illinois, where his remains were buried in East City Cemetery on July 14, 1847 following their return from Saltillo. The funeral of Hardin, a former congressman and commander of the militia unit that had persuaded the Mormons to leave Illinois peacefully, was attended by 15,000 people.[169]

Not surprisingly, the remains of some of the officers who were killed in the battles that occurred in the Valley of Mexico or died during the occupation of the capitol, were disinterred and taken home to the United States for reburial. Among these were six men belonging to the 2nd Regiment of New York Volunteers, namely Lt. Col. Charles Baxter, who died September 17, 1847 of wounds received in the Battle of Chapultepec, Capt. James Barclay, who passed away at San Angel on January 30, 1848, Capt. Charles H. Pearson, who died on October 10, 1847 as a result of the wounds he received at Chapultepec, Lieut. Charles F. Gallagher, who died near Mexico City on September 10, 1847, Capt. Abram F. Van O'Linda, who was killed at Chapultepec on September 13, 1847, and Lieut. Edgar Chandler, who was wounded at Churubusco on August 20, 1847 and succumbed the following day.[170]

The return of the New Yorkers' remains to the "Empire State" was both initiated and arranged by New York City's board of

---

[168] Johnson, p. 127; *Frankfort Cemetery in Kentucky*, 203-204.

[169] Allen, p. 10; *Who Was Who in America, Historical Volume, 1607-1896* (Chicago: A. N. Marquis Co. 1963), 233.

[170] Butler, *Complete Roster of Mexican War Officers*, 72; *Report of the Special Committee...*, 5 & 19.

aldermen, who passed a resolution in November 1847 that at first called for them only to retrieve the remains of Baxter and Chandler, both of whom had been born in the city. The list, it appears, was later expanded to include any officer, volunteer or regular, who had died in the Valley of Mexico and was a New Yorker by birth. To carry out this task, a three-man committee selected one Alexander S. Forbes, age 28, "who personally solicited the agency, and who produced strong recommendations," as their special envoy to Mexico. After the committee obtained from the United States War Department "all the necessary papers pertaining to a mission of this kind," Forbes "proceeded on his errand of humanity" on January 29, 1848, traveling overland to New Orleans, where he arrived on February 9th.[171]

On February 20th, Forbes left New Orleans on a vessel bound for Vera Cruz. He arrived on the 26th, where, reported the special agent in the only letter he ever sent, "I immediately commenced searching for the bodies." Before leaving New York, he reminded the committee, they had received a letter from Col. Ward B. Burnett, commanding officer of the 2nd New York, telling them that Capt. Marsena R. Patrick of the 2nd Infantry Regiment had taken charge of the bodies "and had promised to send them to New York." But when Forbes called on Captain Patrick at Vera Cruz, "he was surprised, and said he knew nothing of them, nor had he promised or spoken to Colonel Burnett on the subject." Notwithstanding the obvious miscommunication, wrote Forbes, Patrick offered to help and within a few days he had found the remains of Colonel Baxter, Captain Pearson, and Capt. O'Linda, who had been brought from Mexico City by Colonel Burnett in January. He also discovered that the bodies of two New York-born regulars, "Captain [Martin J.] Burke [of the 1st Artillery] and Lieutenant [Charles F.] Morris [of the 8th Infantry] had been sent or taken home by their brother officers attached to their respective regiments." After a wagon train from the capitol arrived at Vera Cruz without bringing the body of Lieutenant Chandler, as he had expected, Forbes arranged for the remains of

---

[171] *Report of the Special Committee...*, 4-5.

Baxter, Pearson, and O'Linda to be "properly taken care of until I am ready to return" and then departed for Mexico City.[172]

Following "a long and tedious march of twenty-four days," wrote Forbes, he reached Mexico City, arriving on April 21st. By May 6th, with the help of the army, he had been able to locate the remains of Barclay, Chandler, and Gallagher and was "now ready to return," on the next available wagon train, he wrote, "which I am in hopes will leave here in five or six days."

The remainder of Forbes' journey to have been uneventful but shortly after arriving back at New Orleans, he became bed-ridden with an illness. On June 17th, when Lieut. Robert M. Floyd, an officer of the New York regiment who happened to be in the city at the same time heard that Forbes was staying at the St. Charles Hotel, he went there to see him, "finding him complaining of sea-sickness." Fearing that Forbes' was suffering instead from a "bilious fever," the young officer called a doctor who diagnosed the dread "black vomit." At first, it was thought the unfortunate man would recover but three days after Floyd first found him, Forbes died.

After securing a lead coffin for Forbes' body, Lieutenant Floyd took charge of it along with the coffins of the six men whose remains Forbes had been sent to Mexico to retrieve. Traveling by steamboat and train, Floyd arrived in New York City on July 4th, where, "amid the noise and confusion incidental to the celebration of the day," the coffins, now seven in number, were received with military honors by the "Baxter Blues," a local militia unit.

After the remains had been transferred to mahogany coffins, "each bearing a plate inscribed with the name of its silent occupant, his age, place of birth, cause of death, &c.," they lay in state "under a sable canopy" in New York's city hall. Two days later, a public

---

[172] Ibid; *Daily American Star*, Mexico City, January 28, 1848,1. The *Star* reported that "Colonel Burnett (Lieut. Brower writes from Mexico) is on his way home, having in charge the body of the late Lieutenant Colonel Baxter, together with the bodies of Capt. Pearson, of Brooklyn, and Capt. Van O'Linda, Albany. They are expected to arrive here on Monday or Tuesday of next week and every preparation is being made to receive them."

funeral was held for Forbes and five of the officers whose remains he had brought back from Mexico. (Van O'Linda was buried elsewhere.) As guns were fired at intervals and church bells tolled, the funeral cortege made its way through the streets of New York, accompanied by the New York Common Council and several local militia organizations. Finally, after services at Grace Church, the six men were interred with military honors in their final resting places at Greenwood Cemetery.[173]

Another officer whose body was returned home was Maj. Edward Webster of the 1st Regiment of Massachusetts Volunteers. Webster, son of the distinguished statesman Daniel Webster, died at San Angel on January 23, 1848.[174] A week later, the *Daily American Star*, an occupation newspaper, reported that the officers of the Massachusetts regiment had passed a resolution to "appoint some suitable officer to accompany the remains of the late Major Webster to the city of Boston, to be there placed in charge of the family of the deceased."[175]

---

[173] Ibid, 9-22.

[174] Butler, *A Complete Roster of Mexican War Officers*, 64.

[175] *Daily American Star*, Mexico City, January 30, 1848, 3.

"Monument over the remains of 750 U.S. Soliders, who fell in the Valley of Mexico during the Mexican War"; *courtesy Library of Congress, Washington, D.C.*

Chapter 4
The Establishment of
Mexico City National Cemetery

On September 28, 1850, a little more than two years following the final withdrawal of U.S. troops from Mexican territory, President Millard Fillmore signed an act of Congress approving the appropriation of $10,000 for the purchase of "a piece of land near the city of Mexico, for a cemetery or burial ground, for such of the officers and soldiers of our army, in our late war with Mexico, as fell in battle, or died in and around said city." The cemetery was also intended for "the interment of American citizens who have died or may die in said city."[176] This act, which created the first ever U.S. national cemetery, either on American or foreign soil, also stands alone as the first and only substantial effort that the federal government has ever made to recover the remains of any of the soldiers who lost their lives during the War with Mexico and to memorialize them.

The man chosen by the State Department to carry out the task of establishing the cemetery was the Reverend George Gideons Goss, an obscure figure in American history. All that is known about Goss is that he was a native of Maine who served as a chaplain with Winfield Scott's army in Mexico in 1847 and 1848 and that he performed similar duty in the Union Army during the Civil War. His usual place of residence, apparently, was Washington, D.C.[177]

---

[176] *U.S. Statutes at Large*, vol. ix (Boston: Charles Little & James Brown, 1851), 506.

[177] Francis B. Heitman, *Historical Register and Dictionary of the United States Army*, 2 vols. (Washington: U.S. Government Printing Office, 1903), vol. 1, 466.

Presumably, on account of the somber nature of the mission and because such a person might better command the respect of the Mexicans (and thus hopefully, enjoy their cooperation), State Department officials felt it was more appropriate to appoint a man of the cloth as their agent, rather than a military officer or government official. Goss was selected in particular, wrote Secretary of State Daniel Webster,[178] for two reasons: First, because he had witnessed the burials of the soldiers who were killed in the battles that occurred in the Valley of Mexico and was therefore "acquainted with the places of sepulture," and secondly, because it was felt that his residence there during the occupation qualified him "to aid in the selection and preparation of the land for the proposed cemetery."[179]

In the performance of his duties, Goss was directed by Webster, who had himself lost a son in Mexico during the war,[180] to "consult and act in concert with" Robert Perkins Letcher, the sixty-three year old former governor of Kentucky, who had been appointed United States Minister to Mexico in 1849.[181] Fearing that the government might be overcharged for the land if its intended purpose were known to any potential seller, Webster also cautioned his fellow New Englander "not to allow the object of your visit to be known until the bargain shall have been concluded."[182]

Goss' written instructions, dated December 20, 1850, advised

---

[178] *Dictionary of American Biography*, vol. x, (New York: Chas. Scribner's Sons, 1936 & 1964), 591. Webster became Secretary of State in Fillmore's cabinet, following the death of Zachary Taylor.

[179] National Archives, Records of the Department of State, Diplomatic Correspondence, Mexico, 15:unnumbered.

[180] *Dictionary of American Biography*, vol. x, 590; Steven R. Butler, ed., *A Complete Roster of Mexican War Officers* (Richardson, Texas: Descendants of Mexican War Veterans, 1994), p. 64; *Picayune*, New Orleans, May 15, 1848, 159. Maj. Edward Webster, serving with the First Regiment of Massachusetts Volunteers, died of exposure on January 23, 1848 at San Angel, Mexico. He is not, however, one of the soldiers buried at Mexico City National Cemetery. Major Webster's remains were carried home to Massachusetts and his funeral was held in Boston on May 4, 1848.

[181] *Dictionary of American Biography*, vol. iv, pt. 1, 193.

[182] Ibid.

him further that the government expected that it would take him no longer than six months to accomplish his mission, that he would be compensated at the rate of six dollars per day, and that his "necessary traveling expenses" between Washington, D.C. and Mexico City would also be paid.[183] Given the political and civil disorder that characterized Mexico during the years immediately following the war, the time allotted was wholly unrealistic[184] and, as it turned out, so was the amount of money appropriated.

With a special diplomatic passport and an advance of $500 in his possession, it appears that Goss began his journey to Mexico in late December 1850, shortly after receiving his instructions from the Secretary of State. He also carried a diplomatic dispatch from Webster to Letcher, which advised the elderly Kentuckian of the purpose of Goss' journey to Mexico.[185] The route the former chaplain traveled is unknown but it is not unlikely that he went by steamship from Baltimore to New Orleans, where upon arrival (if he faithfully followed Webster's instructions), he presented his passport to the Mexican Consul for countersigning. From New Orleans, Goss would certainly have booked passage on a steamship to Vera Cruz, a voyage that ordinarily lasted about five days.[186] His next step would have been to take a stagecoach that retraced the overland route followed by Scott's invading army nearly three years earlier, passing through the towns and cities of Plan del Rio, Jalapa, Perote, and Puebla. No doubt Goss was well aware that bandits, who frequently preyed upon unwary travelers on the National Road, posed a particular threat for a *gringo* bearing a large sum of money. One can easily imagine that the intrepid minister took the precaution of hiring one or more persons to accompany him as an armed escort before

---

[183] *Dictionary of American Biography*, vol. iv, pt. 1, 193.

[184] *Harpers' New Monthly Magazine*, vol. ii, no. x, March 1851, 557.

[185] National Archives, Records of the Department of State, Diplomatic Correspondence, Mexico, 15:unnumbered.

[186] This estimate is based on records of some of the various regiments that served in the Mexican War and traveled to and from the United States by steamship.

setting out on the final leg of his journey.[187]

If there are any extant records of Goss' activities while in Mexico, such as letters he wrote to the State Department or that he may have sent to family or friends, they do not easily come to hand. In the absence of such documentation, it is difficult to reconstruct an accurate account of how he went about accomplishing his mission. For the most part, all we have to rely upon are a handful of diplomatic dispatches that were sent to and from the American legation in Mexico City and some brief mention of the cemetery's progress in the *Congressional Globe.*

Goss' arrival in Mexico City probably coincided with the January 15th inauguration of Mariano Arista (the general who had been bested by Zachary Taylor at Palo Alto and Resaca de la Palma nearly five years earlier) as President of Mexico.[188] Perhaps Goss even witnessed the ceremony, which took place on a balcony of the National Palace, overlooking the city's grand plaza (through which Gen. Winfield Scott had ridden triumphantly in September 1847). Certainly, he must have immediately called upon Robert Letcher at the American legation, where he delivered Webster's message to Letcher and at the same time, presented his own credentials. Letcher, for his part, must surely have assisted Goss in locating suitable housing before arranging to meet with the former chaplain once he had rested after his long and no doubt tiresome journey.

Unfortunately, either before or shortly after Goss arrived, Letcher was stricken with an illness, the nature of which is unknown. It was so serious however, that on January 26th, Letcher departed for

---

[187] *Harper's New Monthly Magazine,* vol. xvii, no. xcvii, July 1858, 178-179; Waddy Thompson, *Recollections of Mexico* (New York & London: Wiley & Putnam, 1846), 20. In his reminiscence, Thompson, a former minister to Mexico, told of taking the stagecoach from Vera Cruz to Mexico City in 1842 and of the necessity of arming one's self against the robbers that were known to frequent the National Road, preying upon unwary travelers. A magazine article, published sixteen years later indicated that the situation had not improved. There is no reason to believe that it was any better in 1851, when Reverend Goss made the same journey.

[188] *Harpers' New Monthly Magazine,* vol. ii, no. x, March 1851, 557.

the United States,[189] presumably to recuperate, leaving the newly-arrived special agent in the capable hands of U.S. Consul John Black, a veteran diplomat whose many years in Mexico included several months during the time that the United States and Mexico were at war.

Like Goss, John Black is a little-known figure in American history. Although he enjoyed a long career in the diplomatic service, Black's contributions to his country have been overshadowed by some of the more-celebrated envoys with whom he worked and assisted, such as John Slidell and James Gadsden.

It is uncertain what role Black played, if any, in the accomplishment of Goss' first task, which was locating a suitable site for the proposed cemetery. Certainly, this must have been the least difficult part of the mission. During the American occupation of Mexico City, the remains of several U.S. soldiers had been interred within the bounds of the English burying ground, a Protestant cemetery established several years prior to the war between the United States and Mexico.[190] This graveyard, which is clearly marked on a battle map published shortly after the war, was located at the northern end of the aqueduct that led south to Chapultepec Castle, at the point where the aqueduct connected with the San Cosmé causeway.[191] Since there were already American soldiers buried there, it's not unlikely that Goss had decided, even before leaving Washington, that he would first try to purchase land in this vicinity. Perhaps he even discussed the possibility with Secretary of State Webster, although a particular site is not mentioned in his instructions.

Once the land had been selected, Goss' next step was to find the owner of the property and enter into negotiations with him. This, apparently, took a considerable amount of time and it's not

---

[189] Ibid.

[190] Miller, 68, 70 & 72.

[191] *Battles of Mexico, Line of Operations of the U.S. Army Under the Command of Major General Winfield Scott on the 8th, 12th and 13th of September 1847* [map].

inconceivable that for this portion of the mission, John Black's Spanish language skills and knowledge of Mexican law were essential to its success. Even so, it was not until July 12, 1851, nearly seven months after his arrival in Mexico, that Goss wrote to the State Department in Washington to report that on June 21, he had purchased two acres of land adjacent to the English burying ground, from one Manuel Lopez, for the sum of $3,000.[192] Having expected that both the purchase of land and the re-interment of the soldiers' remains would be completed by that time, at least one official at the State Department was less than pleased. On August 25, shortly after receiving Goss' letter, W. J. Derrick, Acting Secretary of State, wrote to Robert Letcher, who was at that time still in the United States. Complaining that Goss had not "offered any satisfactory explanation of the delay in accomplishing this object" and knowing that Letcher was soon to return to Mexico, Derrick directed the Kentuckian to look into the matter. Furthermore, Derrick wrote: "If...in your opinion he should not have been duly diligent in attending to the business and if any other person can be found there qualified to accomplish it, you will inform Mr. Goss that his services are no longer required."[193]

Despite Derrick's admonishment of Goss, there is no indication that the special agent was ever relieved of his duties. It appears instead that Letcher, upon his return to Mexico sometime during the fall of 1851, discovered that the former chaplain had encountered some unforeseen difficulties. One perhaps, was the unsettled state of affairs in Mexico at that time. In May 1851, a correspondent for *Harper's New Monthly Magazine* reported that Arista's administration "has not thus far realized the anticipations which had been cherished of it [for keeping order]." The result, he declared, was that the "country is infested with predatory Indians and brigands." As an

---

[192] Paul M. Badgely, Superintendent, Mexico City National Cemetery, undated information sheet.
[193] National Archives, Records of the Department of State, Diplomatic Instructions, Mexico, 15:74.

example, he recalled an incident that occurred a few months earlier, when "a train of wagons was attacked in broad daylight, a few miles from the capital, by a band of 15 robbers who drove off the military escort and carried away a large amount of goods."[194] Whether or not this lawlessness hampered Goss' efforts in any way is unknown. Not the least of his troubles, however, was a Mexican law that forbade the exhumation of any remains that had not been buried at least five years. At that time, only four years had passed since the battles occurred in which the soldiers had been killed and in the case of some of those who had died during the occupation of the capital, only a little more than three years had gone by.

For this portion of his mission, it is certain that Goss turned to John Black for assistance. On October 21, 1851, Black wrote to the State Department in Washington, reporting that at Goss' request, he had verbally petitioned the governor of the *Distrito Federalé* to grant special permission for the remains of the U.S. soldiers "interred at various points within the limits of this city" to be exhumed and reburied at the new American cemetery. At the same time, for reasons that are uncertain (but probably at the insistence of the State Department), he requested authorization to remove the bones of General James Wilkinson, the infamous filibuster who died in Mexico in 1825, from their burial place in the church of San Miguel, and to bury them also in the newly-established cemetery. The governor, in turn, took Black's request to the district's board of health, who granted the necessary permission.[195]

The governor's letter, advising Black that consent to the exhumation of the remains had been approved, is dated December 10, 1851. In addition to the church of San Miguel, where Wilkinson was buried, it lists three places where the remains of U.S. soldiers could be found. These were "on the grounds of the Chapel of Saint Anthony near Saint Lazarus, in the immediacy of the Church of Saint

---

[194] *Harper's New Monthly Magazine*, vol. ii, no. xii, May 1851, 849.
[195] National Archives, Records of the Department of State, Diplomatic Dispatches, Mexico, 9:19.

Ferdinand, and the fields near the 'Paseo Nuevo' (New Stroll)." The letter also names a Dr. Rafael Martinez, "who will be paid by the requesters," to perform the exhumations and reburials. In the absence of further documentation, this seems curious. Why wasn't George Goss named in the letter? Does this mean that Goss had left Mexico by this time? Or could it simply mean that the Mexicans wanted one of their own to supervise the work? The answer is unknown.

Whether or not Goss personally supervised the removal of the soldiers' remains from their battlefield graves to the new American cemetery is uncertain. Regardless, he returned to Washington either in late 1851 or early 1852, leaving his mission uncompleted. On March 11, 1852, U.S. Senator James M. Mason of Virginia stood before the Senate and reported that "the remains of some five hundred officers and soldiers, who died from disease or were killed in battle" during the Mexican War had been removed to the new American cemetery in Mexico City. Unfortunately, he noted, "there are probably as many more remaining" who had yet to be re-interred. As a result, said Mason, the Committee on Foreign Affairs was recommending a further appropriation of $3,000 so that "this object should be carried into effect."[196]

By the time he left Mexico, George Goss had incurred expenses that totaled $1,480.34 over and above the original $10,000 appropriation he was authorized to drawn upon. Out of that amount, $3,000 had been spent on land. If we assume Goss remained in Mexico for at least a year, his compensation, at $6 per day, would have come to another $2,190. The amount of his traveling expenses are not known but it is not unlikely that after paying those, he still had about $4,000 to pay for the exhumation and reburial of the soldiers remains plus the walling and ditching of the property. Given the no doubt low cost of employing Mexican laborers to perform that work, it seems that the original amount allotted should have

---

[196] *The Congressional Globe*, New Series No. 45, 32nd Congress, 1st Session, March 12, 1852, 717.

been sufficient. But it wasn't. There are two possible explanations: Either the cost of labor was higher or bribes were paid in order to obtain permission from the federal district's board of health to grant the special dispensation that was necessary before the exhumations could be carried out. Whatever the case, on July 21, 1852, an act appropriating the expenditure of the additional amount Goss found it necessary to spend was approved.[197] A little more than a month later, on August 31st, Congress voted in favor of granting the $3,000 appropriation asked for by the Committee on Foreign Affairs.[198]

The long wait for additional funds to finish the work began in 1851, combined with the presidential election of 1852 and the death of Secretary of State Daniel Webster on October 24th of that same year probably contributed to the government's delay in sending Goss back to Mexico. It was not until February 11, 1853, that outgoing President Millard Fillmore directed Webster's replacement, Edward Everett, to re-appoint Goss "for completing the work as provided for in the Civil and Diplomatic appropriations Act approved 31st August last."[199]

With a letter in his pocket addressed to Alfred Conkling, the new U. S. Minister to Mexico, an advance of $1,000, and a raise in pay to $8 per day, Goss returned to Mexico City, arriving sometime in April 1853. Shortly thereafter, U. S. Consul John Black again interceded on his behalf, in order to obtain a renewal of the permission that had been granted two years earlier for the exhumation of the bodies on account of less than five years having passed since their burial. In view of the fact that by 1853 nearly six years had passed since the battles of 1847, it seems curious that Black found it necessary to seek renewal or indeed, why it would even be required. The only possible answer seems to be that once again, bribes were necessary in order to gain the cooperation of Mexican authorities. Whatever the reason,

---

[197] *U.S Statutes at Large*, vol. x, 21.
[198] Ibid, 94.
[199] National Archives, Records of the Department of State, Diplomatic Correspondence, Mexico, 15:unnumbered.

permission to continue the exhumations was granted on May 30[200] and presumably, Goss was thereafter able to resume his duty. In the end, the remains of a total of 750 U.S. soldiers were removed to the cemetery and interred in a single mass grave. His mission finally accomplished, Goss probably returned to the United States in the late summer or early fall of 1853.

Whether or not Goss had anything to do with the small cenotaph that was erected in the American cemetery shortly after its establishment in 1851-1853 in unknown. Presumably, however, this tribute to the men who were buried there was paid for out of government funds. The earliest known picture of the monument, bearing the inscription "750 Americans" appears in the July 1858 edition of *Harper's New Monthly Magazine.*[201] No mention of it, however, is made of it in the accompanying article. Another engraving, published in the July 1874 issue of *Harper's* shows a different, although similar, monument that bears a stronger resemblance to the one that presently graces the site.[202] Whether this was the second monument to be erected in the cemetery or if the artist who created the earlier picture drew an inaccurate picture is unknown.

An article that accompanied the 1874 engraving had this to say about both the English and American cemeteries in Mexico City:

> If we…walk on up the San Cosme road, we shall come, after a mile or more, to where the aqueduct suddenly wheels westward, and turns its face toward Chapultepec. Opposite this turn you see the shaded gateway of the English cemetery. The American adjoins. Each is neatly kept; but the English has a prettier array of shrubs and trees and flowers, because they take more pains or because they have more wealthy residents here, or because they have a more cultured taste for landscape adorning…Inside the American is a monument to our soldiers who fell before Mexico. It is somewhat touched with

---

[200] National Archives, Records of the Department of State, Diplomatic Dispatches, Mexico, 9:23.
[201] *Harper's New Monthly Magazine,* vol. xvii, no xcviii, July 1858, 179.
[202] *Harper's New Monthly Magazine,* vol. xlix, no. ccxc, July 1874, 178.

time, and needs a little attention on the part of our officials or visitors.[203]

SOLDIERS' MONUMENT IN THE AMERICAN CEMETERY.

Until 1976, this monument bore the following inscription: "To the memory of the American Soldiers who perished in this valley in 1847 whose bones, collected by their country's order, are here buried - 750."[204] In deference to Mexican sensibilities (presumably), the wording has since been changed to read: "To the honored memory of 750 Americans known but to God whose bones collected by their country's order are here buried."[205]

---

[203] Ibid, 178-179.

[204] *The Mexico City Post*, Mexico City, June 29, 1940.

[205] Monument to Mexican War dead, U.S. National Cemetery, Mexico City. The problem with this new wording, obviously, is that by making no reference to the war or to the fact that the 750 Americans were soldiers, a casual observer may wonder, perhaps, how such a large number of people came to die and be buried in that place. By including the words "known but to God," the inscription

In addition to the 750 American soldiers who were buried there during the period 1851-1853, some 813 civilians who died in Mexico City between 1851 and 1924 were also interred in the American cemetery at San Cosmé, along with several post-Mexican War servicemen. Some of the civilians were veterans of the Mexican War, the Civil War (both Union and Confederate), Indian campaigns, and the Spanish-American War of 1898. Others were members of the U.S. diplomatic corps, or their families. The first non-Mexican War burial was of a man named Reuben Willhite, who passed away in Mexico City on November 20, 1851. The last, it appears, was a U.S. Army hospital steward, Charles Knowlton Sams, who died December 14, 1923.[206]

For reasons unknown, it appears that the remains of Gen. James Wilkinson, who was supposed to have been reburied in the American Cemetery during the time that George Goss supervised its establishment, were not moved to the site until 1872.

Appropriately, perhaps, the first caretaker of the American cemetery was a veteran of the U.S.-Mexican War. His name was James Wright. During the occupation of Mexico City, apparently, Wright married a Mexican *señorita* with whom he had fallen in love. When the war was over, the former sergeant elected to remain in his wife's country, afterward going by the name of *Santiago* Wright. His initial compensation is unknown but on May 18, 1872, when Congress appropriated $500 to reimburse the American consul for the cost of maintaining the "American Protestant Cemetery" for the past year, it also approved a annual salary of $1,105 for the cemetery

---

also gives the impression that the names of the deceased are unknown. While it is surely true that that no individual remains could be identified, the names of the soldiers who were killed in battle or died during the American occupation of Mexico City are recorded in both casualty lists and muster rolls. They are not "unknown soldiers."

[206] The American Battle Monuments Commission, "Mexico City National Cemetery," undated information sheet, and hardcopy of computerized list of interments in the Mexico City National Cemetery, dated January 5, 1981.

keeper.[207]

Not surprisingly, when Caretaker Wright died in 1877, he was buried in the cemetery he had tended for more than twenty years. When his wife Eulalia passed away in 1899, she too was buried there.[208]

In 1873, the American cemetery in Mexico City was officially declared a national cemetery, to be operated and maintained by the War Department. In 1947, President Harry S. Truman signed an executive order transferring responsibility from the War Department to the American Battle Monuments Commission, which had been created following the First World War. Today, in addition to the Mexico City National Cemetery, the Commission maintains twenty-three other U.S. cemeteries around the world.

The remains of all the people buried in the Mexico City National Cemetery lay undisturbed and relatively forgotten until 1976 when construction began for a new highway called the *Circuito Interior*. At that time, the property was reduced in size to a single acre. The civilian remains were exhumed and re-interred in crypts constructed at the east and west walls of the grounds by the Mexican government. Simultaneously, the remains of the 750 American soldiers were re-interred in two new vaults placed in the center of the south end of the grounds.

Today, the cemetery forms a tiny oasis of calm and quiet in the heart of Mexico City. It is located behind high walls at Virginia Fabregas 31, Colonia San Rafael, near the intersection of San Cosmé and Melchor Ocampo. The *Plaza de la Constitución*, or *Zocalo*, is about 2½ miles to the east and the U.S. Embassy is about 1 mile south.[209]

---

[207] *U.S. Statutes at Large*, vol. xvii, p. 124.

[208] *The Mexico City Post*, Mexico City, June 29, 1940; The American Battle Monuments Commission, hardcopy of computerized list of interments in the Mexico City National Cemetery, dated January 5, 1981.

[209] The American Battle Monuments Commission, "Mexico City National Cemetery," undated information sheet; *American Memorials and Overseas Military Cemeteries* (Washington, D.C.: The American Battle Monuments Commission, 1989), 2.

Not unlike the war which caused it to come into existence, the cemetery is little known and rarely visited. In the fall of 1997, however, around the time of the 150th anniversary of the fall of Mexico City, two small groups of Americans separately visited the site in order to pay homage to the soldiers who lie buried there. One was a collection of historians and "history buffs" who had signed up for an organized tour that took them from Vera Cruz to the capital, along the route of Scott's march. The others were members of the Aztec Club of 1847, descendants of some of the officers who had formed the society 150 years earlier during the American occupation of the Mexican capital. In both instances, prayers were offered, speeches were made, and wreathes were laid at the base of the tiny monument that marks the site of the mass grave.[210]

---

[210] Richard Breithaupt, *Aztec Club of 1847, Military Society of the Mexican War: Sesquicentennial History, 1847-1997* (Universal City, California: Walika Publishing Company, 1998), 146-148.

Chapter 5
The Monterey and Saltillo Investigations

Although the bodies of several officers and even a few privates were returned to their homes for reburial, most of the soldiers who died in Mexico (apart from those removed to the cemetery in Mexico City) remained buried in their original graves, knowledge that troubled the National Association of Veterans of the Mexican War. In 1874, when the organization was first formed, one of its declared objectives was: "To rescue from oblivion the memory of their comrades who died and were buried on the battle-fields of Mexico, and to procure the official publication, by the Government, of their names in a Roll of Honor, and proper care bestowed on their resting place." That same year, the organization sent a request to the War Department, inquiring about the condition of the graves of their fallen comrades who had been buried at Monterey and Saltillo. What they learned would probably have mortified Captain William S. Henry, who died in 1851 and was thus spared any knowledge of what had become of the little cemetery so lovingly constructed and cared for by the soldiers of the 3rd Infantry Regiment.[211]

In response to the veterans' request, the War Department directed United States diplomatic officials at Monterey and Saltillo to investigate and file a report. In due course, J. Ulrich, the U.S. consul stationed at Monterey, composed a letter which painted a less-than-encouraging picture. It read, in part:

The men who were killed at the taking of Monterey were buried at the place where they fell, some below the town, near the tanneries, others near the 'Obisprado' [sic] (Bishop's Palace,) and some of the

---

[211] Heitman, vol. 1, 524.

officers who were killed, and some officers and men who died were buried near the Walnut Springs, where General Taylor had his camp. At the latter place, there was, at one time, an inclosure, and some stones marking some of the graves. At present there is no indication on the spot of its having been a burial place, corn being planted there, and the stones probably now being in the walls of some of the ranchitos in this vicinity. At none of the places where there were burials are there now any signs to mark the spot, and there are few persons here who could identify them...There are no monuments of any kind whatever.[212]

At the same time his counterpart in Nuevo León was attempting to ascertain the condition of American graves at Monterey, U.S. Consul A. G. Carothers was conducting a similar investigation at Saltillo. In the report that he wrote afterward, Carothers noted that the bodies of U.S. soldiers who died from wounds or from disease during the nearly two years that the city was occupied, "were buried in a vacant lot contiguous to the old Campo Santo, of this city, on the southeast side of town." The site, called the "Campo Santos de los Americanos," was afterward enclosed, reported Carothers, "and the graves were at one time marked by stones." Unfortunately, he added, the land on which the burial ground was established was private property and "the American officers neglected to procure a title to it." Consequently, Carothers explained, "the owner has, many years since, reclaimed his land, and destroyed every vestige of its being a burial place. A short time since a crop of corn was harvested from this lot, and it is now planted in wheat."[213]

Whether the site he described in his report was the same burial ground where many of the U.S. officers were interred in 1847 or a different place is unclear. In either case, Carothers knew that the aging veterans had hoped not only to acquire this burial ground but also to gather the remains of their comrades buried at other places in

---

[212] A. M. Kenaday, *Proceedings of the National Assocation of Veterans of the Mexican War, Second Annual Reunion Held in the City of Washington, February 22d and 23d, 1875* (Washington: John H. Cunningham, Printer, 1875), 29.
[213] Kenaday, 29.

the vicinity of Saltillo, to reinter them in one spot, and to erect a memorial of some kind on the site. Consequently, the intrepid consul visited the Governor of Coahuila, who "freely offered to do all in his power to protect [a marker] from defacement in the event of its erection, providing that it be simply a memorial monument, and contains in its inscriptions nothing of a triumphal character, calculated to offend the sentiments of the Mexican people by reference to their discomfiture in the battle." The consul also added his opinion "that the [Campo Santos de los Americanos] could be purchased, for a small sum, from its present owner, and the title deeds registered in the proper office." This belief and the governor's assurances notwithstanding, however, Carothers offered his recommendation that because of "the uncertainty…of their identification, and the almost impossibility of collecting them in one place, as well as the remote localities in which the bodies are interred, and the consequent difficulty of guarding [a marker] against unauthorized, willful defacement, I would respectfully suggest that the most feasible thing to be done is to erect a suitable memorial monument in the Camp Santo…of this place, purchasing the necessary ground from the…municipal authorities." "It would thus be secured from all depredation," he added, "and from the public character of the places better carry out the idea of showing the nation's gratitude to its illustrious dead." Carothers further suggested that the same thing be done in Monterey and that the monuments for both places either "be made in the United States from iron and shipped here" or "be made from a very fine marble which can be procured near Matiula, in the State of San Luis Potosi, 60 leagues from here."[214]

Given the discouraging nature of these reports, it is easy to see why the National Association of Veterans of the Mexican War, after receiving them, failed to take any further action. With their small numbers and their no doubt equally limited finances, the old soldiers apparently deemed it more important to try to push for passage of

---

[214] Ibid.

federal legislation that would grant service pensions to elderly survivors of the war, instead of efforts to memorialize their fallen comrades. In pursuance of the former goal they were successful, although it took thirteen years, from 1874 to 1887, to achieve it. The latter ambition, although never fully abandoned, was not achieved.

In 1897—the 50th anniversary of the Battle of Buena Vista— Thomas T. Crittenden, U.S. Consul-General at Mexico City (himself a U.S-Mexican War veteran), sent a letter to Senator G. G. Vest of Missouri that sparked a second federal investigation into the condition of the American graves at Saltillo. In this letter, Crittenden enclosed a newspaper clipping that "if wholly true," he wrote, "is somewhat mortifying to the American citizens here."[215]

The article sent by Crittenden, published in an unnamed newspaper, was entitled "The United States Should Look To It." It read:

> On February 23, 1847, the anniversary of Washington's birthday, the battle of Buena Vista was fought near the city of Saltillo, and a number of the United States soldiers are buried in a quasi reservation. For a number of years an adobe wall protected the last resting place of these soldiers, but this has now fallen down. A wagon road traverses a number of the graves, and, sad to relate, the washing of rains has unearthed portions of skeletons, which are bleaching in the sun. It does seem as if the Federal Government of the United States could make some arrangement with the Mexican authorities and protect the last resting place of the dead.[216]

On June 3, 1897, in response to Crittenden's letter and the newspaper clipping he had sent, Senator Vest offered a resolution on the floor of the Senate that called for "the Secretary of State...to cause immediate inquiry to be made as to the facts and communicate the same to the Senate, with such recommendation as he may deem proper." It was adopted, apparently, without dissension or debate.

The following day, a directive was sent from the Department of

---

[215] *Congressional Record*, vol. 30, pt. 1, 55th Congress, 1st Session, 1897, 1435.
[216] Ibid.

State to John Woessner, the U.S. Consul at Saltillo. Upon receipt of this missive, Woessner reported in a dispatch dated June 21, "I immediately visited the place where, it is said, the American soldiers who were killed at the battle of Buena Vista February 27 [sic], 1847, are buried." His description of the site was no less disheartening than the one his predecessor had written more than twenty years earlier:

> Regarding this burial ground, I have to state that it is a lot about 300 feet square, situated on the east side of this city. The old adobe wall around it is in a very bad condition, in parts completely down, leaving open places where animals and people pass over it. There are no bones exposed to the weather and no signs or any indications of it having been a burial place, except the old adobe wall around it.[217]

Although "some of the old inhabitants here inform me that this lot I mention is the place where our soldiers were buried who were killed at the battle of Buena Vista, and also some of our soldiers who died in the hospital at Saltillo a short time afterward," Woessner was not certain he had visited the correct site. To assure himself, he wrote, "I addressed a communication to the governor of this state [Coahuila]...asking him to inform me the actual condition of this burial ground, and also to furnish me with a certified copy of the titles to same." He also suggested that "an examination of the records of the years 1845 to 1848 in the War Department at Washington, D.C., might be of valuable assistance relating to this burial ground and its titles."[218]

The governor of Coahuila, Miguel Cárdenas, was remarkably cooperative. In July, after receiving Woessner's letter, he directed the municipal president of the city of Saltillo to carry out an inspection of the U.S. burial ground. His report, prepared on July 17, 1897, and passed on to Woessner by Cardenas on July 19, disclosed:

---

[217] National Archives, Records of the Department of State, Consular Dispatches, Saltillo, Mexico, 1:79; U.S. Congress, Senate, *Graves of the American Soldiers Near Saltillo, Mexico*, 55th Cong., 1st sess., S. Doc. 180, 2.
[218] Ibid.

That in the year 1846 this City was occupied by the military forces of the army of the United States, the Chief of same ordered raised or built a mud wall, the ruins of which still exists, in front of the Grave Yard of this City, situated on the East side, and in which are buried the various bodies of the Chiefs or Officials and Soldiers of such of their respective Company, who died a natural death. Afterwards in Feby. and March 1847, in a piece of uncultivated land of an irregular shape outside of the enclosed square and adjoining, were buried a considerable number of bodies of the soldiers who were killed in said battle referred to, without the knowledge of the Municipal authorities, perhaps owing to the state of alarm existing in this City at that time. After the evacuation of this City by the American forces in the said year of 1847, the land owners and Municipal corporation made use of their lands, recovering their property without, neither before nor afterwards, fencing nor laying it off nor designating it as a Grave Yard or Cemetery.[219]

Going beyond the call of duty, the Mexican official who inspected the site included with his report a hand-drawn plan or map of the burial ground that clearly indicated that it was located beside an arroyo or creek and was crossed in the center by two streets, the *Calle Antigua* and the *Calle Nueva*. Owing to the slope of the land on the side adjoining the arroyo, he explained that "the washing of the soil or other causes" had caused some bones to be uncovered from time to time. These, he added, had been "deposited in the Charnelhouse of the principal Grave Yard of this City."[220]

On August 3, 1897, Woessner sent a second dispatch to the State Department, enclosing the map of the burial ground and the results of the governor's investigation. He also advised that if the government intended to purchase the property, that any negotiations with the land owners "should be carried on very quietly in order to avoid the sellers from asking for it an exorbitant or excessive price." Property in the vicinity, he remarked, was "worth [only] moderate prices." In closing, Woessner declared that if the government hoped

---

[219] National Archives, Records of the Department of State, Consular Dispatches, Saltillo, Mexico, 1:79.
[220] Ibid.

to take the matter further, he would "take great pleasure in placing my best services, at the disposition of the [State] Department, to acquire [the lot]" and have it "beautified to a worthy degree."[221]

Woessner's reports were forwarded by the State Department to the Senate, which published them as Senate Document No. 180 but for some unknown reason, no further action was taken.

In 1900 a third investigation into the condition of the U.S. burial ground at Saltillo was conducted by a Colonel Scully of the United States Army's Quartermaster Corps, who was sent to Mexico in response to reports that the graves of U.S. soldiers were being desecrated. On July 31st, Colonel Scully wrote to the Adjutant General's office in Washington, D.C., recommending that "These remains be removed to the San Antonio, Texas National Cemetery where they can be decently and revently [sic] interred and cared for." As with earlier reports, however, it appears that nothing more was done.[222]

In 1965, an American visiting Mexico found a cemetery in Monterey that fit the description of the one established by the 3rd Infantry. It was located "in the vicinity of Ojo Nogal, just west of the old road to Marin," although all the headstones were said to be of Mexicans. This could be explained, it was conjectured, by "the old Mexican practice of disinterring the dead," which it made it "seem likely that the American soldiers' bodies were gradually displaced over the intervening years." The author of the book in which this information appeared, speculated that "the growth of the city and the amount of new construction in this vicinity of Monterey" had probably obliterated any trace of this site that he believed contained "the graves of foreign invaders."[223]

The same person who found what he thought was the 3rd Infantry's cemetery in Monterey in 1965 also visited Saltillo. There,

---

[221] Ibid.

[222] Chance, *Franklin Smith*, 244, n. 27.

[223] Chance, *Franklin Smith*, 243, n. 27; Lawrence R. Clayton and Joseph E. Chance, eds., *The March to Monterey: The Diary of Lt. Rankin Dilworth* (El Paso, Texas: Texas Western Press, 1996), 70-71.

he found the wall surrounding the U.S. burial ground in downtown Saltillo had been destroyed, but that "the old foundation [was] still visible." He also noted that: "Other walls made of adobe from materials on the spot have numerous human bones visible and easily removed with a knife or screw driver."[224]

Curiously, none of these investigations included the grave sites of the approximately 267 soldiers buried at Buena Vista Battlefield. According to one modern-day writer, the burial ground is located at the Coahuila Agriculture Station, which occupies the former site of the Hacienda Buena Vista (for which the battle was named).[225]

---

[224] Ibid.

[225] Ibid. In Mexico, it is *La Angostura* (the Narrows).

Chapter 6
U.S. Government Policy Since 1898

There is no doubt that the U.S. soldiers who died during the U.S.-Mexican War of 1846-1848 have been singularly neglected by the government that they served. Notwithstanding the establishment of Mexico City National Cemetery and the later investigations of American burial grounds at Monterey and Saltillo, no attempts have been made by the United States, apparently, to either retrieve the remains of the majority of soldiers buried in Mexico, to secure titles to their burial places, or even to erect a national monument in Washington, D.C., commemorating their service to the nation. In contrast, the remains of soldiers who died during subsequent foreign wars, as well as their families, have been the beneficiaries of federal laws and regulations that reflect a humanitarian spirit and awareness that seems not to have existed at the time of the U.S.-Mexican War.

On July 8, 1898, at the height of the Spanish-American War, President William F. McKinley approved an act of Congress "making appropriations to pay session employees of the House of Representatives, and for other purposes." Included in the act was a section authorizing the sum of $200,000 to "enable the Secretary of War, in his discretion, to cause to be transported to their homes the remains of officers and soldiers who die at military camps or who are killed in action or who die in the field at places outside of the limits of the United States."[226]

Two years later, Congress not only appropriated a further $100,000 for the same purpose but also passed a law that allowed the families of any soldier who had died "while on duty away from home" since January 1, 1898, and whose body was "taken home and

---

[226] *U.S. Statutes at Large*, vol. xxx, 730.

buried at the expense of the family or friends of the deceased," to "be repaid at the expense of the United States," provided that the cost did not exceed what it "would have cost the United States to have transported the remains to their homes."[227]

During the Spanish-American War, which lasted approximately six months, a little more than 306,000 soldiers served on active duty. This was nearly three times the number who had participated in the U.S.-Mexican War. Out of the former group, there were 2,446 deaths (385 combat, 2,061 other) or less than 1 percent of the whole. In contrast, nearly 12% of all the U.S. troops who served in the War with Mexico died in service.[228]

Because the Spanish-American War was so short in duration, most soldiers never had the opportunity to leave the United States. Consequently, the number who died on foreign soil was also very small.[229] No doubt even fewer, thanks to the law passed by Congress in July 1898, were buried outside the United States.

In 1919, immediately following World War I, federal legislators broadened the policy they had begun a little more than two decades earlier by appropriating more than $8 million to transport to their homes the remains of officers, U.S. military academy cadets, surgeons, and enlisted men, to pay for the interment of deceased soldiers in national cemeteries, to move the remains of soldiers buried at abandoned posts to permanent posts or national cemeteries, and to reimburse individuals for the cost of "burial or shipment of the remains of officers or enlisted men of the Army who die on the active list," provided the expenses were incurred after July 1, 1910.[230]

A year later Congress approved the spending of an additional $21 million for the same purposes, as well as for the "expenses of the

---

[227] Ibid., 1224-1225.

[228] "Statistical Summary, America's Major Wars," The United States Civil War Center website (www.cwc.lsu.edu/other/stats/warcost.htm).

[229] Graham A. Cosmas, *An Army For Empire: The United States Army in the Spanish-American War* (Shippensburg, Pennsylvania: White Mane Publishing Co., 1994), 244, 266 & 278.

[230] *U.S. Statutes at Large*, vol. xli, 84.

segregation of bodies in permanent American cemeteries in France." A provision in the same act allowed $1,000 for "repairs and preservation of monuments, tablets, roads, fences, and so forth, made and constructed by the United States in Cuba and China to mark the places where American soldiers fell."[231]

In 1923, Public Law No. 534 created the American Battle Monuments Commission, which is still in existence today. It consists of seven members appointed by the President of the United States, including one officer of the United States Army to serve as the group's secretary. In 1923, the commission's first task was to "prepare plans and estimates for the erection of suitable memorials to mark and commemorate the services of the American forces in Europe and erect memorial therein at such places as the commission shall determine, including works of architecture and art in the American cemeteries in Europe."[232]

During the First World War, of the nearly 5 million U.S. citizens who served in the military forces of the United States, 136,516, or a little less than 3%, lost their lives. Another 4,452, or less than one-tenth of one percent, were reported as "missing-in-action." To accommodate the remains of the 30,921 deceased soldiers whose next-of-kin elected to have their loved one's remains interred in Europe rather than have them shipped home, eight overseas U.S. cemeteries were established—one in England, one in Belgium, and six in France. The largest is the Meuse-Argonne American Cemetery near Verdun, where more than 14,000 U.S. soldiers are interred.[233]

Between 1941 and 1945, more than 16 million U.S. citizens donned military uniforms to serve in the Second World War. Of that number, 405,399 died in service and 77,245 were classified as "missing-in-action." Nearly three-fourths of the accountable fatalities were combat-related deaths. Presumably, most of the MIAs were also

---

[231] Ibid., 895-896.

[232] *U.S. Statutes at Large*, vol. xlii, 1509.

[233] U.S. Battle Monuments Commission website (www.usabmc.com/abmc44.htm).

the result of enemy action. Notwithstanding such large numbers, however, the odds of getting killed in the Second World War were no greater than for the First. Between 1941 and 1945, the number of Americans who died in service or were listed as MIA again amounted to less than 3 percent of the whole.[234]

Of those whose bodies could be found, 93,242 were buried in fifteen U.S. cemeteries located overseas, the establishment of which was authorized by Public Law 368, approved August 5, 1947,[235] or in a national cemetery located on the Hawaiian island of Oahu. If the MIAs are included, the number whose remains were not brought home to the United States account for less than 20 percent of the combined number of MIAs and deaths in service. For the First World War the number whose bodies were not brought home was a little more than 22% if the MIAs are also included.[236]

Since the end of World War II, no U.S. military cemeteries have been established overseas. All the 54,246 Americans who lost their lives in Korea between 1951 and 1954 and all the 58,168 who died in Vietnam during the 1960s and early 1970s, whose remains could be accounted for, were either shipped home or interred in the national cemetery at Honolulu, Hawaii. None of the less than 300 servicemen or women who died during the Gulf War and whose remains can be accounted for, have been buried overseas either.[237]

Over the years, Congress has become more generous. In 1954, when Public Law 495 renewed the federal government's commitment to assuring that the remains of deceased soldiers were brought home from overseas, it also allowed payment for "(a) notification to the next of kin or other appropriate person; (b) recovery and identification of remains; (c) preparation of remains for burial…; (d) furnishing of a casket or urn, or both, with outside box; (e) hearse service; (f) funeral director's services; (g) transportation of remains

---

[234] Ibid., (abmc45.htm).

[235] *U.S. Statutes at Large*, vol. 61, part 1, 779-880.

[236] American Battle Monuments Commission website, (abmc44.htm).

[237] Ibid., (abmc46.htm & abmc47.htm).

and an escort of one person, including round-trip transportation and prescribed allowances for such escort, to the town or city, or national or other cemetery, designated….; (h) furnishing of a uniform or other articles of clothing; (i) presentation of a flag of the United States to the person recognized as the one to direct the disposition of the remains…; and (j) interment of remains."[238]

Today, the families of deceased U.S. military personnel are still entitled to the benefits authorized by law in 1954. For the next-of-kin of soldiers who have died since 1961, the government has also paid the "necessary expenses of a memorial service" for any deceased soldier whose remains "are determined to be unrecoverable."[239]

---

[238] *U.S. Statutes at Large*, vol. 68, part 1, 478.
[239] *United States Annotated Code*, Title 10: Armed Forces (The West Group, 1998), 864.

Soldiers' graves, Arlington National Cemetery; author photo.

Chapter 7
Conclusion

The evidence is indisputable: There is a striking difference between the federal government's "non-policy" regarding deceased military personnel during the U.S.-Mexican War and the more compassionate measures that have been put into practice since 1898. What is difficult to understand is why so little effort was ever made to address the disparity, particularly during the late nineteenth century when the war was still within living memory, when Mexican War veterans were anxious to see their fallen comrades honored, and when it might have been a simpler task to locate and obtain title to U.S. burial sites in Mexico than it would be today, or to retrieve soldiers' remains and return them to the United States.

Why the majority of deceased soldiers were left buried in mostly unmarked graves in Mexico in the first place is something modern-day U.S. citizens, unaccustomed to such a seemingly irresponsible and unfeeling attitude on the part of the government, may find difficult to comprehend. After all, weren't these men in the service of the United States when they died? Did they not have families whose lives were forever changed by the loss of a husband, a father, or a son? Would it have not been some comfort to them to have their loved one's remains returned home so that the fallen soldier's grave could be visited or failing that, to know that he rested in some spot that was suitably marked and cared-for by a grateful nation? The answer to all these questions, of course, is yes. Then why was this particular group of American military personnel, the first to fight and die on foreign soil, treated with such apparent indifference when future troops who would die under similar circumstances were not?

To those who have knowledge of the conditions under which

armies operated in the field during the early nineteenth century, the answer seems obvious. Tradition, founded upon considerations of health and common decency, required that the corpses of battle fatalities be interred as quickly as possible. The effects of decomposition, many a soldier has written, are unpleasant, offending both the eyes and the nose. After the Battle of Buena Vista, wrote Pvt. Benjamin Scribner, "The scent from the field was almost insupportable."[240] At Cerro Gordo, another soldier told of the horror of seeing dead Mexican *soldados*, "their bodies…drawn up and stiffened in convulsive movements."[241] The sight of large numbers of dead men, whether the victims of a battle or disease, could no doubt be demoralizing to troops. It was simply in the best interest of the army to dispose of the dead as quickly as possible.

Although tradition may account for why soldiers who died in Mexico were buried there, it does not explain why they were left behind when the war was over. If the government could transport soldiers' remains back to the United States from Cuba, Puerto Rico, and the Philippines in 1898, why could it have not done the same fifty years earlier in 1848? The answer, it seems, is that men who served in Mexico simply "died too soon."[242]

It is important to recall that when the war began in 1846, there were people still alive who could remember when George Washington was president. The United States was still something of an experiment. The notion that the national government had a humanitarian obligation to its citizens, something that modern-day U.S. citizens take for granted, was alien to those who lived in a simpler age. When the men who volunteered to fight in Mexico in 1846 and 1847 marched off to war, they did so with no assurances of any kind that their remains would come home or that their graves would not be abandoned. In all likelihood these soldiers did not

---

[240] Scribner, p. 70.

[241] Allen, p. 599.

[242] It should be pointed out the U.S. policy at this time was no different, apparently, than that followed by Great Britain, France and other countries.

expect anything different nor did their families.

This view of limited government seems to have been shared by those who made the laws of the land. If federal legislators had believed otherwise, surely an act of Congress mandating better treatment of the remains of deceased soldiers would have been passed much earlier in the nation's history.

The lack of such legislation might also be explained by the haste with which the United States entered into the war as well as the equally slap-dash way it was conducted. In 1846, fighting on foreign soil was a new experience for the United State Army. Contrary to the view that President Polk had purposely provoked the conflict, when Captain Thornton's dragoons were ambushed at *Rancho de Carricitos*, the United States government was also caught off guard. General Taylor's inability to move his troops for nearly three months during the summer of 1846 for want of supplies and transportation is but one example of how unready the U.S. was to wage a war with Mexico. The failure of Congress to legislate a policy regarding the remains of deceased soldiers between 1846 and 1848 may have been another result of this almost scandalous lack of planning and preparation.

Notwithstanding that the United States Army left nearly 13,000 dead American soldiers in Mexico when it withdrew in 1848, the government's establishment of Mexico City National Cemetery three years later makes it clear that members of Congress felt it was appropriate for the nation to demonstrate that it had not forgotten those men who sacrificed their lives. What is puzzling is why the government's efforts stopped short by honoring only those who died while serving with Scott's forces in the Valley of Mexico, a number that amounted to less than six percent of the whole.

One possible explanation has ironic overtones: Under the terms of the Treaty of Guadalupe Hidalgo, a vast new expanse of land was added to the United States. One of the immediate effects of this "Mexican cession" was to open a debate in Congress that focused on whether slavery should be allowed in any part of the newly acquired territory. The Compromise of 1850, which admitted California as a free state also allowed the residents of any other states formed out of the former Mexican lands to decide for themselves whether to allow slavery. This averted civil war, at least for a time, but in 1854, the year following George Goss' return from Mexico, the Kansas-Nebraska Act reopened what became, as the 1850s progressed, an increasingly bitter sectional debate. With Congress distracted by this controversy, honoring dead soldiers in Mexico no doubt soon became a matter that would have to wait. In other words, by winning the war, the soldiers who fought and died in Mexico became the instrument of their own neglect by creating a situation that diverted the attention of those who had the power to honor them.

This may explain why Mexico City National Cemetery was the government's only attempt to honor its fallen soldiers from the War with Mexico during the decade that preceded the Civil War, but what about after? Why did Congress not take care of its obviously unfinished business once the bloody struggle between the North and South was finally finished?

Again, the answer seems to be that federal legislators were distracted with more pressing matters. The abolition of slavery and the "Reconstruction" of the South were two of the most immediate concerns. Apparently, so was establishing national cemeteries in the United States for the interment of the remains of fallen Civil War soldiers, a much larger group and much closer to home than those who lay in their unmarked graves in faraway Mexico. The old adage, "out of sight, out of mind," seems certainly to have applied in their case. Politics no doubt also played a role in the neglect. During the years that immediately followed the Civil War, the Republican Party dominated Congress. The Republicans were the successors to the Whigs, the party whose members had been most vehemently opposed to the War with Mexico. American politics in the nineteenth century was no less partisan in nature than today. Doing something to honor soldiers who had died in what they no doubt viewed as a Democrats' war seems hardly likely to have been at the top of the

Republican Party's post-Civil War agenda.

If Mexican War veterans ever held out any hope that federal legislators would take some appropriate action to "to rescue from oblivion" their comrades who had lost their lives in the war, it was struck a hard blow by the Civil War. Not only was Congress afterward dominated for many years by a party unsympathetic to their concerns, Mexican War veterans henceforth had to compete for attention against Civil War veterans, who numbered approximately 3½ million in number—North and South combined.[243] Veterans of the Mexican War, in comparison, numbered only about 97,000 men at the close of their particular struggle. By 1874, when they first organized on a national level, these old soldiers probably numbered less than 40,000. With such a small force, the "Heroes of '46" faced an uphill battle in their attempts to persuade the government to honor the memory of "our long neglected brothers whose mortal remains have occupied unmarked graves in foreign soil for more than a quarter of a century."[244]

The Mexican War veterans' lack of political clout is probably best exemplified by their 13-year struggle, which began in 1874, to persuade Congress to pass a bill authorizing an $8 per month service pension for survivors or widows. Not surprisingly, one of the largest obstacles to the success of this effort were Republican legislators, particularly those who represented Northeastern states, who seemed more concerned in the costs of such an act than easing the financial burden of men who pressed their claim on the not-unfounded basis that their victory had greatly enriched the nation. "Our country has been called on," NAVMW president James W. Denver told his fellow veterans, "to give recognition of your services; services unsurpassed in the magnitude of their results to the whole people, and the glory of our arms, by any other army in modern times." "It cannot be," he

---

[243] The Editors of Time-Life Books, *Brother Against Brother: Time-Life Books History of the Civil War* (New York: Time-Life Books, 1990), 414 & 418.
[244] .*Proceedings of the National Association of Veterans of the Mexican War, 2nd Annual Reunion*, inside front cover & 19.

concluded, "that your appeal will remain long unheeded by Congress."[245]

But once again, the Civil War presented a problem. Notwithstanding that a significantly large number of Mexican War veterans were no doubt residents of northern states, some Republican congressmen were opposed to any legislation that would grant federal pensions to men who had served the Confederacy, as some Mexican War veterans had certainly done. The most conspicuous of these, of course, was Jefferson Davis, the former president of the Confederate government. During the War with Mexico, Davis had had served as colonel of the 1st Regiment of Mississippi Rifles and had been wounded at the Battle of Buena Vista while serving under his former father-in-law, Zachary Taylor. It no doubt helped the Mexican War veterans' cause when Davis, in a letter to Congressman Otho B. Singleton of Mississippi, stated that he would renounce any claim to a Mexican War service pension if it would aid his old comrades-in-arms in their effort to obtain one.[246] A Democratic majority in the House, during the first administration of President Grover Cleveland, no doubt also made a difference when the bill was finally passed and signed into law on January 26, 1887.[247]

It might be supposed that their protracted struggle to obtain a service pension was one reason why survivors of the Mexican War, the only group of Americans who seemed to have any interest in the matter during the late nineteenth century, did not more actively press Congress to authorize the retrieval of the remains of their fallen comrades from their graves in Mexico. Another, certainly, was because even the old soldiers began to wonder about the feasibility of such a course of action. The results of the 1874 investigations of U.S. burial sites in Monterey and Saltillo had obviously discouraged the veterans. No doubt they feared that any monuments they put up in

---

[245] Ibid, p. 34.

[246] *Proceedings of the National Association of Veterans of the Mexican War, 5th Annual Reunion* (Washington, D.C.: 1878), 40.

[247] *U.S. Statutes at Large*, vol. 24, 371-372.

Mexico might be defaced or worse perhaps, that marking the sites could result in the desecration of American graves by embittered Mexicans, thus pointing up the government's bad judgment in allowing the bones of its soldiers to remain buried in what had been enemy soil. "It is perhaps not practicable to render proper tribute to the memory of these men on the soil where they were buried, within the jurisdiction of another government," wrote NAVMW president James W. Denver in 1875, "nor is it likely, after the lapse of so many years, that their remains could be gathered up for burial here in their present state of dissolution." As an alternative proposal that echoed the sentiment of people who believed Mexico might be better off under the U.S. dominion, the NAVMW passed the following resolution:

> Resolved. That in the opinion of this Association, the erection of monuments at Monterey and Saltillo, in honor of those American soldiers who fell in the War with Mexico should be postponed until that country shall be annexed to the United States but that, in the meantime, a proper monument ought to be erected near the Capital of the United States.[248]

Although veterans of the Mexican War achieved their goal of obtaining a service pension, attempts to persuade Congress to erect a monument honoring their fallen comrades did not enjoy similar success. That effort persisted, however, for another two decades until the old soldiers finally realized that "old age, physical disabilities and poverty" had made it "impossible for us to pursue the enterprise of building a monument to our war with Mexico." Nevertheless, they were determined to do something before they died that would stand as tangible evidence of their service and the sacrifice of those who failed to return home from the war. Seizing upon the preservation of battlefields as an alternative, the Texas Association of Veterans of the Mexican War, at its 1907 reunion in Dallas, passed a resolution that

---

[248] *Proceedings of the National Association of Veterans of the Mexican War, 2nd Annual Reunion*, 30.

called upon them to purchase the battleground at Palo Alto and donate it to the State of Texas so that it could be "maintained in a manner worthy of the event it commemorates."[249] They also had an interest in the preservation of the original Fort Brown earthworks but neither plan came to fruition. It would be another 85 years before Congress would belatedly authorize the inclusion of Palo Alto Battlefield in the United States National Park system. As yet, only private organizations and the State of California have tried to preserve any other Mexican War sites in the United States.

Bad timing was probably another obstacle to gaining the government's interest or cooperation in any efforts to memorialize the soldiers who died during the War with Mexico. In 1876, shortly after the first investigations of U.S. burial sites in Mexico were conducted, a second U.S.-Mexican War was nearly provoked by outlaws who crossed the border into the United States to raid U.S. settlements and then fled back to safety in Mexico. In 1877, although the Mexican government called it "a serious offense to the national dignity and the sovereignty and independence of Mexico," U.S. forces made a dozen forays into Mexican territory in an effort to bring the raiders to justice. In September 1877, American soldiers came close to clashing with regular Mexican troops at the village of Zaragoza. This strained relationship between the two countries must surely have contributed to any doubts that both the veterans and the United States government might have had regarding the cooperation of Mexican authorities, which would have certainly been needed for any efforts to obtain title to U.S. burial grounds or retrieve soldiers' remains to be successful.

The government's failure to adopt the recommendations made by the men who reported on the condition of the American burial ground at Saltillo in 1897 and 1900 may also have been the result of bad timing. In 1898, war broke out with Spain, with fighting in the Philippines for a further two or three years. Once again, it seems, the government was distracted by more pressing matters.

---

[249] *Daily Dallas Times Herald*, May 18, 1907, 10.

With no living veterans to press the issue, it is hardly surprising that during the twentieth century no effort whatsoever, apparently, was ever made by the United States government to fulfill what one nineteenth century writer referred to as its "national duty" to the forgotten soldiers of the War with Mexico. Overshadowed by popular interest in the Civil War, the earlier conflict has all but vanished from the national consciousness. What amounts to a case of national amnesia has no doubt contributed to a lack of action. If the majority of Americans have forgotten the war, can federal legislators be blamed for being equally ignorant of it? Although the majority of writers have assigned equal blame to both countries, a growing trend among historians to portray the struggle between the United States and Mexico as an immoral war certainly has not helped.

Finally, the question must be asked: Will anything ever be done? At this point in time, it seems unlikely. If ignorance of the war or the belief that it was a disreputable episode in American history are not sufficient obstacles to prevent any future action by the government, the current relationship between the United States and Mexico might certainly be a barrier. The relationship has always been somewhat strained, oftentimes coming close to the breaking point. In 1914, U.S. troops, for the second time in less than a century, occupied the Mexican port city of Vera Cruz for a period of time and in 1916, as in 1877, U.S. troops were sent to the border to protect American lives and property threatened by Mexican raiders. Even today, although the two nations maintain a superficial cordiality, a certain amount of tension exists. How to deal with drug smuggling across the U.S.-Mexican border is but one of several sore points, with both sides feeling that the other is not fully cooperating. It is also true that despite the millions of dollars that U.S. tourists spend at Mexican resorts each year, many Mexican citizens view their northern neighbors as brash and arrogant and unlike most Americans, the people of Mexico still remember, and are embittered by what they term the "*Yanqui* Invasion of 1847." Aware of these sentiments, the United States government seems to have taken great pains in recent years to demonstrate sensitivity to Mexican concerns. The changing of the wording on the monument in Mexico City National Cemetery, to eliminate any reference to the war, is but one example. In the 1990s, during a trip to Mexico, President Clinton laid a wreath at the *Los Niños Heroes* monument, a memorial to the celebrated Mexican cadets who lost their lives fighting U.S. troops at the Battle of Chapultepec. If the President placed a similar tribute at the grave of the seven-hundred-and-fifty U.S. soldiers who are buried nearby, it went unreported.

Presently, the only groups that seem to have an interest in calling attention to the federal government's neglect of U.S. military personnel who died during the U.S.-Mexican War are two national lineage societies: The Aztec Club of 1847, whose members are descended from officers only, and the Descendants of Mexican War Veterans, a Texas-based society whose members are descended from enlisted men as well as officers. Beginning in 1995, the latter organization made some tentative attempts to find a congressional sponsor for a bill that would authorize the erecting of a national Mexican War memorial in Washington, D.C. The DMWV, however, was, and still is handicapped by the same shortcomings that hampered similar efforts by its predecessor, the National Association of Veterans of the Mexican War, namely a small membership roll and limited funds. As a consequence, after about six or seven years, the group gave up. Meanwhile, the society continues to try to increase the public's awareness of the U.S.-Mexican War by maintaining an Internet website devoted to the history of the conflict and also publishes books and a quarterly journal.[250] Several members contributed articles to an encyclopedia of the U.S.-Mexican War, published by Macmillan and Company in 1998.[251] Whether these

---

[250] Steven R. Butler, *Origins and Progress of the Descendants of Mexican War Veterans, 1989-1999* (Richardson, Texas: Descendants of Mexican War Veterans, 1999).

[251] Donald Frazier, ed., *The U.S. and Mexico at War* (New York: Macmillan and Co., 1998). DMWV members who contributed articles to this work were Steven R. Butler, Joseph E. Chance, Harwood P. Hinton, David D. Jackson, William J.

activities will strengthen the organization's ability to rescue the "forgotten soldiers" from the oblivion into which they seem to have disappeared still remains to be seen.

Schultz, Linda D. Vance, Bruce Winders, and Kevin R. Young.

The Taking of Monterey, September 1846; from Benson J Lossing, *Our Country: a Household History for All Readers from the Discovery of America to the Present Time*, Volume Two (New York: Ames Publishing Company, 1888).

Epilogue

I am very happy to report that on Wednesday, October 27, 2016—some seventeen years after the chapters in this book were originally written—for the first time since the middle of the nineteenth century, the remains of U.S. troops that died in the War with Mexico were repatriated to their homeland.

These remains, consisting of the bones of from eleven to thirteen American soldiers—believed to be Tennessee volunteers—were flown from Mexico, at U. S. government expense, to Dover Air Force Base (in Delaware), where they were received with full military honors. From there, they were taken to Middle Tennessee State University (MTSU) in Murfreesboro, to be examined by forensic scientists and historians, such as Professor Hugh Berryman of MTSU and Professor Tim Johnson of Lipscomb University in Nashville, who had worked since 2009 with both Democratic and Republican congressional representatives and U.S. diplomats to bring these men home at last.

Some of these remains were discovered in 1996 by builders in Monterrey. Others were uncovered later. The process of repatriation was slow in part because Mexican officials wanted to be sure that the remains were definitely the bones of American soldiers, and not Mexicans, before allowing them to leave the country. Artifacts found on the discovery site reportedly convinced them. Although identification of individuals is not expected, Berryman, who is the lead scientist of the investigation, reportedly hopes to learn, among other things, how these men died. Once all the forensic tests are complete, it is expected that the remains of these soldiers will be then be interred at the Gallatin City Cemetery in Gallatin, Tennessee, where there is already a U.S.-Mexican War memorial on site.

It is believed these soldiers may be among the troops who fought for control of an old tannery on September 21, 1846 during the Battle of Monterey (as it was then spelled).

Although the repatriation of these remains is good news for anyone concerned about such matters, this appears to be a singular event, since there is still no official federal government effort to systematically track down and repatriate the remains of soldiers who died in the War with Mexico.

Here are the names of the Tennessee Volunteers who died in battle at Monterey:

Capt. W. B. Allen.
2d Lt. S. M. Putnam.
Pvt. J. B. Porter, Co. C.
Pvt. Wm. H. Robinson, Co. C.
Sgt. John A. Hill, Co. D.
Pvt. B. F. Coffee, Co. D.
Pvt. E. W. Thomas, Co. E.
Pvt. B. H. Dolton, Co. F.
Pvt. I. Gurman Elliot, Co. G.
Pvt. P. H. Martin, Co. G.
Pvt. Edward Prior, Co. G.
Pvt. Benj. Soaper, Co. G.
Pvt. Henry Collins, Co. H.

Pvt. Jas. H. Allison, Co. I.
Pvt. Jas. H. Johnson, Co. I.
Pvt. Jas. B. Turner, Co. I.
Pvt. R. D. Willis, Co. I.
Pvt. J. B. Burkitt, Co. K.
Pvt. J. M. L. Campbell, Co. K.
Pvt. A. J. Eaton, Co. K.
Pvt. A. J. Gibson, Co. K.
Pvt. Finlay Glover, Co. K.
Pvt. A. J. Pratt, Co. K.
Pvt. Wm. Rhodes, Co. K.
Pvt. John W. Sanders, Co. K.
Pvt. G. W. Wilson, Co. K.

About the Author

Steven R. Butler is a founder and past president (1989-2001) of The Descendants of Mexican War Veterans and a former editor of *Mexican War Journal*. He earned his M.A. and Ph.D. in History from the University of Texas at Arlington. Presently, he is an Associate Professor of History at Collin College in Plano, Texas and an Adjunct Professor of History at Richland College in Dallas, Texas.

www.ingramcontent.com/pod-product-compliance
Lightning Source LLC
LaVergne TN
LVHW021351080426
835508LV00020B/2219